TWO BY O'HARA

JOHN O'HARA

TWO BY

O'HARA

The Man
Who Could Not Lose
AN ORIGINAL SCREEN STORY

Far From Heaven
A MELODRAMA

HARCOURT BRACE JOVANOVICH
BRUCCOLI CLARK
NEW YORK AND LONDON

Contents

Foreword

It has been a long time for those of us who thought that John O'Hara (1905-1970) would provide at least one book a year in perpetuity. *TWO by O'Hara* should bring back memories of the years when the yellow sheets were coming out of his typewriter every night and there was a new O'Hara book published on Thanksgiving Day.

Between the publication of his first *New Yorker* story in 1928 and 1970, when he died with page 74 of a novel in his typewriter, O'Hara published 402 short stories or novellas and thirteen novels—a body of work unsurpassed in scope and fidelity to American life. Beginning with his first novel in 1934, *Appointment in Samarra*, he wrote five of the best American novels—including *A Rage to Live, Ten North Frederick, From the Terrace*, and *Ourselves to Know*.

One of the remarkable things about the O'Hara canon is that most of it was written in his fifties, after he quit drinking in 1953 and married Katharine Barnes Bryan in 1955. At the time of life when most American writers have completed their best work, O'Hara began his most productive period with a brilliant five-year burst of books: *Ten North Frederick* (1955), *A Family Party* (1956), *From the Terrace* (1958), *Ourselves to Know* (1960), *Sermons and Soda-Water* (1960). It is also remarkable that he mustered the strength to work on journalism, screenplays, and drama as well as novels and stories. He loved to write; it became impossible for him not to write. His pleasure in the mastery of his craft was intensified by a compulsion to preserve the things that he believed he knew better than anyone else. Haunted by mortality, he wrote against the last deadline. As he explained in *Imagine Kissing Pete* (1960), "I

Foreword

missed almost nothing, escaped very little, and at fifty I had begun
to devote my energy and time to the last simple but big task of
putting it all down as well as I could."

Inevitably, O'Hara left unpublished work at his death. Some
of it was unfinished; some of it was not intended for publication;
and some of it was ready for publication. The two previously
unpublished works paired in this volume are not major O'Hara.
But they are by John O'Hara and merit publication as examples of
his work in genres other than the novel and story, for he was proud
of his professionalism—his ability to meet certain standards in
everything he wrote.

The Man Who Could Not Lose (1959) and *Far From Heaven*
(1962) were written during John O'Hara's most productive
period—the great harvest that began with *Ten North Frederick* in
1955 and yielded eighteen more books by the time of his death in
1970. Why did O'Hara interrupt his novels and stories to work on
speculative projects? Not for money at this point. The answer must
be sought in his ambition to enlarge his achievement. Having
commenced what was virtually a new career, he may have wanted
his comeback to include successes in all the genres he had
previously attempted. Although he remained cynical about the
Hollywood system, he was aware that he had never been
responsible for the screenplay of a major movie. And, despite many
attempts, none of his straight plays had reached Broadway.

The Man Who Could Not Lose and *Far From Heaven* both
examine the effects of isolation, though from different approaches.
The theme of isolation—or call it loneliness—may well be the
main theme in O'Hara's work. He observed in *We're Friends Again*
(1960), "What, really, can any of us know about any of us, and why
must we make such a thing of loneliness when it is the final
condition of us all? And where would love be without it?" Again
and again, his heroes discover that they are alone—without love—
and the recognition is unbearable. Julian English commits suicide

Foreword

in *Appointment in Samarra*; Joseph Chapin deliberately drinks
himself to death in *Ten North Frederick*; Robert Millhouser
marries a corrupt girl more than thirty years his junior in
Ourselves to Know.

THE MAN WHO COULD NOT LOSE

Beginning in 1934 John O'Hara worked on some twenty movies,
usually as a "polish guy"—revising the dialogue in other
writers' scripts. *Moontide* (1945), an ambitious disappointment,
was the only movie for which he received sole screen credit—and
even this screenplay was revised by producer Mark Hellinger.
Although critics charged during the Thirties and Forties that
O'Hara had been spoiled by Hollywood, he insisted that he did not
take movie work seriously because he could never work well under
the collaborative system of movie writing. He did not try to join or
beat the system and was careful not to be deflected from his real
work.

In 1955, at the same time that he was writing *Ten North
Frederick*, O'Hara was at Twentieth Century-Fox working on the
original screen story for *The Best Things in Life Are Free*. The
musical biography of the DaSylva-Henderson-Brown songwriting
team was produced from a screenplay by William Bowers and
Phoebe Ephron after O'Hara declined to stay on in Hollywood and
adapt his screen story. He wanted to return to Princeton and
concentrate on novels. A deal was subsequently made whereby
O'Hara would work at home on three movies for Twentieth
Century-Fox—for $75,000 each. The first of these was an
adaptation of Frank O'Rourke's western novel, *The Bravados*, in
1955-1956. O'Hara's screenplay was rejected, and the movie was
made from a screenplay by Philip Yordan. At the suggestion of
David Brown, who was in charge of creative material at the studio,
O'Hara was then asked to write originals in any form. *The Man*

Foreword

Who Could Not Lose was written in 1959. Another screen story called "The Matadors" was never completed.

O'Hara had hoped that Alfred Hitchcock would be available to direct *The Man Who Could Not Lose*; but the project never developed beyond the original story because Twentieth Century-Fox was thrown into chaos in 1960 by the death of Buddy Adler, the head of production. Brown's comment is that *The Man Who Could Not Lose* languished through "default, inadvertence, and lethargy."

The form of *The Man Who Could Not Lose* is not a treatment or a screenplay: it is a skeletal novel. In 1960 O'Hara explained to his friend Brown:

> When I wrote THE MAN WHO COULD NOT LOSE, *even* when I was writing something for the eyes of a small and special group who are themselves technicians, I was determined to get away from the Hollywood practice of writing a screen original so that even Jack Warner would understand it. I get so bored with writers who hate to write. They have a very good reason for hating to write; they're in the wrong business.[1]

The Man Who Could Not Lose examines a man whose cold intelligence cuts him off from emotional nourishment. Since Martin Ziegler is self-isolated, he is not destroyed by the absence of love. He is a survivor. Indeed, he is more than a survivor. Yet for O'Hara life without emotion—without love—is not worth living. Even if love is doomed, the pains of love gone bad—and it frequently does go bad in O'Hara—are preferable to its absence. The man who could not lose is, clearly, a big loser.

[1]*Selected Letters of John O'Hara*, ed. Matthew J. Bruccoli (New York: Random House, 1978), p. 336.

Foreword

FAR FROM HEAVEN

The history of John O'Hara's stage projects was long and frustrating. He worked on at least sixteen plays—not all of which were completed.[2] With the splendid exception of his book for the *Pal Joey* musical in 1940, none of his plays reached Broadway. Only two, *The Farmers Hotel* (1946-1947) and *The Searching Sun* (1952), received try-out performances. O'Hara blamed the producers' lack of interest in his plays on his refusal to rewrite or to allow his work to be doctored by other writers. Even after he had given up on Broadway, he continued to write plays—usually in the spring—claiming that it was his way of unwinding after completing a novel. The 1961 publication of *Five Plays* (*The Farmers Hotel, The Searching Sun, The Champagne Pool, Veronique,* and *The Way It Was*) was probably intended to generate production interest in them. If so, the plan did not work.

Despite his genius with dialogue, O'Hara was a storyteller—not a playwright. The techniques of his novels and stories were not transferable to the stage, which lost the background and details that provided the life of his fiction. It is meaningful that O'Hara converted two of his plays into novels: *The Farmers Hotel* was novelized in 1951, and *The Sisters* was published as *Elizabeth Appleton* in 1963.

O'Hara finished *Far From Heaven* at 12:45 A.M. on 17 March 1962. It is one of his three best plays—with *Pal Joey* and *The Farmers Hotel*—and the only one of the three that was never published or produced. *Far From Heaven* was written with Jackie Gleason in mind for the role of John J. Sullivan. When Gleason

[2]See Bruccoli, *The O'Hara Concern* (New York: Random House, 1975), pp. 210-211 for a list of John O'Hara's plays.

announced his retirement from the stage, O'Hara made no attempt to have the play produced. But he did not abandon it. In 1963 he offered the play to *The Saturday Evening Post* for conversion into a story. Since no one at the magazine was brave enough to undertake the job, O'Hara planned to "reconstitute" the play himself but didn't. At about the same time he considered adapting the play into a musical, with a score by Howard Dietz and Arthur Schwartz, as a vehicle for Mary Martin "if she wants to change from those greasy kid parts."[3] Nothing came of this project.

Far From Heaven presents a familiar O'Hara figure: the man confronted with the deprivation of admiration, respect, and what he accepts as love. It is hardly news that John O'Hara was openly sentimental in life as well as on paper; but his sentimentality was not fraudulent. It was an earned emotion developed from his susceptibility to acts of loyalty or generosity or kindness—and from his painful sensitivity to acts of cruelty. O'Hara acknowledged the sentimentality of *Far From Heaven* by designating it a melodrama, but it is also a drama of redemption. Nevertheless, John J. Sullivan is not a tragic figure, and the play is not a "Sullivan Agonistes." From first to last his heaven consists of long shots, graft, compliant women, a tailor-made Tux.

The art of fiction is primarily the art of character creation, and Sullivan is utterly convincing (more so than Ziegler). Given O'Hara's method of character creation, Sullivan's psychological pattern was undoubtedly based on someone O'Hara had known, though the action was invented. In this way O'Hara tried to achieve what he called "God's truth, out of life."[4] Although it would be hyperbolic to claim that only John O'Hara could have made us pity Sullivan, a gauge of *Far From Heaven* is the degree to which it compels an unwilling involvement with Sullivan.

[3]*Letters*, p. 421.   [4]*Letters*, p. 402.

Foreword

This is the epitaph on John O'Hara's gravestone in the Princeton Cemetery:

Better than anyone else, he told the truth about his time, the first half of the twentieth century. He was a professional. He wrote honestly and well.

O'Hara did not select his epitaph, but the words were his own self-appraisal made in a 1961 interview. No great effort of imagination is required to hear him saying, "That's telling them!"

Matthew J. Bruccoli

Editorial Note: The texts of *The Man Who Could Not Lose* and *Far From Heaven* have been printed from John O'Hara's own typescripts. Punctuation and spelling have been conservatively emended; but O'Hara's words have not been changed except as noted.

The Man Who Could Not Lose

AN ORIGINAL SCREEN STORY

ABOVE
John O'Hara with his Rolls-Royce
Silver Cloud III

OPPOSITE
John O'Hara in his study
at "Linebrook," Princeton, New Jersey

OVERLEAF
John O'Hara aboard the Queen Mary

1

The very blonde girl in the yellow swimming suit got up from the sand and detached herself from the beach party. She walked to the edge of the water and stood looking out over the sea.

In a few minutes she was joined by one of the young men of the party. "Why do you do that?" he asked.

"Do what?"

"This is the third time you've left the rest of us, and all you do is stare out at---at what?"

"That island."

"What's so fascinating about the island?"

"I don't know," she said. "As far as that goes, what's so fascinating about that little group?"

"I can't argue with you on that. I guess they bore me as much as they do you."

"They're your friends. You shouldn't say that."

"Maybe that gives me the right to say it. I know them, and you only met them today."

"And will never see them after tomorrow."

"Or me either?"

"I suppose so."

"I want to see you again."

"Why?"

"I don't know. But I do."

"Not very likely, though. In another week I'll be back in Chicago. And in two more weeks I start teaching kindergarten."

"Is that what you do?"

"It's what I'm going to do. I haven't yet."

"Well, in two more weeks I'll be back at law school."

TWO BY O'HARA

"Is that what *you* do? I wondered."

"You did? Why?"

"Because you're the only one in that group that seemed to have any purpose in life. The others---nothing."

"There you are, staring out at your island again."

"My island?"

"Well, hardly yours. The French call it the Island of the Cedars, officially. But they have another name for it. It's known as Ziegler's Island. They call it that because an old crook named Ziegler moved there years ago. He was running away from the law back home. Let's go over and have a look at it."

"You mean swim it?"

"No. Hire a boat."

"All right. I'll go halves with you."

"No, you won't. I'm loaded."

Together they went to the wharf and hired a sailboat with a kicker from a man who obviously knew the young man.

"They know you," said the girl.

"They ought to. I'm a good customer. This is my third summer at this place. But do you know something? As many times as I've hired this boat, I've never sailed to Ziegler's Island."

"Why not? Any reason?"

"Yes, sort of. My grandfather was clipped for plenty by Old Man Ziegler, and I've always thought of the island as enemy territory."

"Then let's not go."

"No, I'd like to. I guess I always wanted to."

It was a five-mile sail to the island. They did little talking, but worked well together in the handling of the boat. "You know about sailing, huh?" he said.

"Did you ever hear of Lake Michigan?" she said. "I've sailed boats all my life."

"Let's tie up over there?" he said, indicating a wharf.

"How about over there?" she said, pointing to another.

The Man Who Could Not Lose

"Okay," he said.

They tied up at the place she had chosen, stepped out of the boat and headed for the village.

"Have you any money? Because I haven't," he said.

"I thought you were loaded."

"I meant my family are. I have credit over on the mainland, but here they don't know me."

"It's all right. I have some money."

"I'll pay you back."

"What are we going to need it for?"

"To hire a car, and drive around the island."

"Oh. That's a good idea."

They hired a broken-down Citroen and drove about the island. "You don't talk much, do you?" he said.

"Don't I?"

"No. In the boat you hardly said a word. Are you always like this?"

"I'm not *always* like *anything*. I like to sail, so why talk? And I'm enjoying our ride."

"Except that I'd like to get in some conversation. And you're going away tomorrow. You're going to have to prattle away when you teach kindergarten."

"Then let me save the prattling till I start."

He was rebuffed, but took it in good spirit. "You know something? You're the most attractive girl I've met all summer."

She was not paying any attention. The winding road had taken them nearly to the top of a hill. At the very top was a large villa amidst a profusion of trees and flowers, and the whole estate was surrounded by a high wall.

"I give up," he said.

"What?"

"I *said*, I give up. I just paid you the compliment of the year, and you're on Cloud 90."

TWO BY O'HARA

"Sorry."

"Not a bit. You're not a bit sorry. Have you got a guy back home? Are you going steady?"

"I hate that expression."

"So do I, but it had one desirable effect. It got a rise out of you."

They had come to the main gate in the wall. "Would you mind stopping here?"

He stopped the car, and she got out, went to the gate alone, and saw that it was securely locked. She returned to the car.

"Doesn't look as if anybody lived there," he said. "But I imagine it's Old Man Ziegler's hideout."

"Shall we go back now?"

"Whatever you say. It's your money."

"It is my money, too. I insist on paying for this part. You can pay for the boat, but I'll pay for the car."

"Considering the fact that I might as well have been somewhere else, all right. You can pay for the car."

They returned to the garage in the village, and an elderly mechanic whom they had not seen before came to wait on them. "I'm returning the car," the young man said in French. "We've had it for two hours. How much do we owe you?"

The mechanic casually looked at the girl, turned to the young man, then suddenly looked again at the girl. "X thousand francs," he said, still looking sideways at the girl.

The girl reached in her bag and handed the money to her companion, who paid the mechanic. They left the garage, and as they strolled through the village it became noticeable that many people stared at the girl, some for her blonde beauty, but among the older natives, those past fifty, there was something besides admiration in their stares. This special curiosity grew, until some of the older people, buzzing among themselves, actually followed the girl and her companion, and the young couple became conscious of it, hastened their steps until they got to their boat and got under way.

"Your name *is* Libby Stanley, isn't it?"

"Yes. Why?"

"Well, I might as well tell you, I've been developing a theory about you. Do you want to hear it?"

"All right."

"Your curiosity about the island, and those people's curiosity about you. And I just noticed something else. If we had tied up this boat where I wanted to, we'd be high and dry now, wouldn't we? Yes. So you knew something about the tides here."

"All right. What's your theory?"

"You've been here before."

"Yes."

"You've lived here. The natives recognized you."

"They thought they did, but they didn't recognize *me*. They thought I was my mother."

"You have lived here, then?"

"I was born here. In that villa on the top of the hill."

"The one I said belonged to Old Man Ziegler."

"It did. Martin K. Ziegler. He was my grandfather."

2

Early in the evening of an autumn day in 1922, in the mainland town where the beach mentioned earlier is situated, a large black Renault limousine, shades drawn, arrived at the wharf. A heavy-set man of forty-five got out and was greeted respectfully by a well-dressed Frenchman. The man, who was Martin K. Ziegler, rapidly exchanged a few words with the Frenchman, and then spoke to his wife and twelve-year-old daughter, who had remained in the limousine. They got out and the three Zieglers and the Frenchman walked the few steps to the wharf, where an express cruiser was tied up, engines throbbing. The party of four boarded the cruiser, which immediately got under way, headed for the island.

Waiting for them on the island was a cabriolet, to which were hitched a pair of horses. The party of four got in the carriage and were quickly driven to the villa on top of the hill. The main gate was closed after they had driven through, and at the door of the villa three servants were on hand to assist with the few pieces of luggage.

"Say goodnight to your father," said Dorothy Ziegler, when she and the others were inside the house.

"Goodnight, Father," said the sleepy child.

"Goodnight, Josie. You've been a very good girl, very good," said Martin Ziegler. He kissed her, and she went off with her mother.

Martin Ziegler turned to the Frenchman. "And while I'm handing out bouquets, you deserve one, Paul."

"Not at all, sir."

"Everything was right on the dot. The way I like things to be. Sit down, Paul."

Paul seated himself stiffly, obediently but not comfortably, while Martin Ziegler remained on his feet.

"You have been working for me, what? Three years?"

"Three years, sir, and two months, I am happy to say."

"It's been a satisfactory arrangement for both of us, I'd say."

"Extremely so for me, sir, and I trust for you as well."

"Don't worry. It has been, or it wouldn't have lasted three years. But now, unfortunately, it must come to an end."

The Man Who Could Not Lose

The Frenchman was shocked. "But, Mr. Ziegler. . . ."

"Don't you know why I'm here? Haven't you guessed the reason behind all the secrecy?"

"I did not allow myself to guess. You have often been---mysterious---but I have learned not to ask questions."

"So you have. But within a week they're going to be asking you questions---"

"They?"

"Yes, they. Paul, I am a fugitive. I am about two weeks ahead of the police. In about two weeks, actually less than that, the New York police will be looking for me, and they are going to be bitterly disappointed to find I'm not there."

"The police?"

"Yes. If I had stayed in New York I would be put in prison. I'm forty-five years old, I've made and lost several good-sized fortunes. But this time---in plain language, I am a crook."

"No, I refuse to believe that."

"You're going to believe it before long. And so I am sorry to say, you have executed your last commission for me." He reached in his pocket and took out a note-case. "Thank you for what you've done in the past three years, and especially the last two weeks. You've earned this money, even if right now it may seem a little dirty."

"I have confidence in you, sir. The utmost."

"You're very kind and very polite, Paul. But there is nothing more you can do. I have plenty of money. I saw to that, you can be sure. But you must get a brand new start."

Paul thought a moment. "Are you planning to stay here?"

"For the rest of my life."

"I could be your agent. No one would know."

"Of course they would. If you began buying a stock everybody'd know you were buying for me."

"Perhaps."

TWO BY O'HARA

"You've been in on some big things, Paul. I think you'll be all right."

Paul nodded and rose. The men shook hands and Paul departed.

3

Martin Ziegler stayed on his island. There was no local aristocracy, and he became a combination of squire and duke, benefactor and patron. His money was his power from the beginning, but with the passage of time the islanders went from cynical tolerance (since they knew he was a fugitive) to an attitude of friendly respect (since he was generous but not foolish). His daughter Josephine was sent to school in Switzerland, and on her vacations on the island she brought home friends whose parents were not unmindful of the fact that Martin Ziegler, isolated on the island, was nevertheless a successful trader in the world financial markets. Men of finance visited him on the island, singly and in groups that included high military figures, recognizable as such in spite of their mufti. There were splendid parties, attended by men and women from the yachts that anchored off the island. Martin Ziegler installed the island's first wireless station on his land, and used it for the well-being of the natives as well as for his own purposes. From the terrace he could swing his telescope about to command a view of the sea and the shipping of the sea, and one day, through the telescope he identified a warship as a U. S. cruiser. He learned that aboard it were several hundred midshipmen from the Naval Academy, and he dispatched an invitation to them to come ashore for a lawn fete. His messenger returned to the villa. "The captain says there is no answer," said the messenger.

But such snubs were rare, and so long as they did not affect

The Man Who Could Not Lose

Josephine, he bore them with some amusement. "What else could they do?" he asked his wife, when the captain of the cruiser refused to reply to his invitation. "There would have been hell to pay if they'd come to my house."

But Dorothy Ziegler was not happy on the island. She was free to come and go; to Paris, to London, to parties on the mainland. She was a handsome woman, had style, but she was sensitive to her situation. Home, which had once been New York, was now a villa on top of the highest hill on a Mediterranean island. It was what she always had to come back to after her trips to London and Paris--- where, indeed, she was never quite allowed to forget that she was the wife of Martin K. Ziegler, with all its unpleasant connotations. She was entertained in the houses of her husband's financial acquaintances, but the wives made no great effort to hide the fact that entertaining her was a duty dictated by the husbands' relationship with Martin Ziegler. Martin, on the other hand, was taking his situation with good humor, and he actually enjoyed his life on the island. "When I was a boy I saw enough snow to last me a lifetime. Minnesota's the coldest state in the Union, and it's lucky my ears didn't fall off in those winters," he would say. He could shoot birds on their way to Africa for the winter; he could swim in his pool; he could ride about the island on horseback; he could read; he could eat and drink as he pleased; and as he said only too often, the world now came to him.

It came to him one day in the person of Francis T. Blackwell, a man who was slightly older than he.

"Martin, I'm frank to confess, I'm surprised you consented to see me," said Blackwell.

"Why shouldn't I see you, Frank? I have nothing against you."

"But I have, against you."

"Oh, I know that," said Martin Ziegler. "But I didn't ask to see you, remember. You asked to see me."

"It doesn't embarrass you to see me?"

TWO BY O'HARA

"Not if it doesn't embarrass you, old man."

"You're incredible."

"Yes, that's the way you'd see it. What have you got to offer?"

"I came because I have reason to know you've made a lot of money since you've been here."

"Yes, I have."

"Then why don't you make good? If you did you'd be able to come home."

"Home, Frank? This is home. I can do everything I want to do right here."

"Not quite everything."

"What can't I do, for instance?"

"You can't leave."

Martin Ziegler was stung by the truth of the remark. "Maybe not," he said. "But *you* can."

"And will," said Blackwell.

"And you can tell the boys back in Wall Street and State Street that you failed."

"That *I* failed? You're the one that was given the chance to redeem yourself. You're the one that failed, Martin, and no one knows it better. I was one of those that trusted you, and the boys back home didn't send me. I came myself, on my own initiative. But now I can't get away from you fast enough."

"Well, try," said Martin Ziegler.

At that moment Dorothy Ziegler appeared. "Why, Frank, how nice. Are you going to stay with us?"

"No, Dorothy, I'm not."

"Frank has been offering me a chance to redeem myself, but I've become such a hardened criminal, I turned him down. Tell me this, Frank. When I ran away six years ago, if I had asked you to lend me four million dollars would you have done it? That was what I needed at the time."

"Not under the circumstances."

The Man Who Could Not Lose

"You don't know the circumstances."

"Ah, but I do. You had got in so deep that it would have taken that much money to get you out."

"Yes."

"You were afraid to go broke, so you took money that didn't belong to you, and you ran away. You've used that money to get rich again. I had hoped that you'd want to pay it back and be able to face people, the people you used to know. But I was wrong."

"Yes, you were wrong. Because I knew none of you would help an upstart like me. You'd all been waiting for exactly the thing that happened."

"Not all of us. If you'd taken your beating like a man there were some of us that would have helped you get a new start. I was one of them, and I think I proved that by coming here, six years later. But now I never want to see you again, and Dorothy, I'm only sorry that you had to hear this."

"If you want to turn this into a social visit with Dorothy, you won't mind if I excuse myself," said Martin Ziegler. He departed.

"I'm sorry, Frank. How is Elizabeth? I've never written to any of our old friends. You can imagine why."

"Elizabeth is well, thank you. She's busy with preparations for the wedding. Our son John."

"Little John getting married. A nice girl, I'm sure."

"Very fine girl. Boston. I'm sorry I won't be seeing Josephine. How is she?"

"Quite grown up. In England at the moment. I wish she could go home, but. . . ."

"Why can't she?" said Blackwell.

"She has no friends at home. Six years at this age. You lose touch, especially when you're that young."

Blackwell had no desire to get into a long conversation with Dorothy Ziegler, one that had already become awkward. "Well, we often think of you."

TWO BY O'HARA

"Thank you, Frank. Give my love to Elizabeth."

"I will, I certainly will," said Blackwell, departing without committing his wife to anything.

Dorothy Ziegler saw him to the door, then walked to the swimming pool. "I suppose you were rude to him," she said.

"Blunt. You can't be rude to a fellow like him. At least I can't be. They're the rude ones. People like me are blunt. Rudeness is an aristocratic privilege, haven't you noticed that in your mingling with the nobility?"

"I haven't noticed anything of the kind."

"Then I've been wasting my time, resenting their rudeness to you."

"They haven't been rude to me."

"Well, the men haven't."

"Oh, dear."

"Yes, oh dear. Where are you off to next?"

"Austria."

"Ah, yes. Von Lemnitzer. The Count Von Lemnitzer. He is teaching you to shoot. All those years I wanted to teach you, you could have been a good shot by now. How long this time?"

"Two months."

"Oh? Does the season last that long?"

"I'm not going to be in Austria all the time."

"It's nice of you to tell me that. I didn't enjoy it when one of my Italian visitors told me he had met you in Rome, and I was under the impression you were in Scotland."

"Do you care?"

"Less and less. But I don't think Josephine likes it very much."

"You don't really know what Josephine thinks."

"Do you?"

"In some things. I know she wants to get married. She has the man picked out. You didn't know that."

The Man Who Could Not Lose

"No, I didn't. Who is he?"

"His name is Philip Stanley, and you won't like him. That's why she hasn't told you."

"But I wonder why she did tell you."

"Because Josephine is like me, no matter how much you try to change her."

"If I believed that, I *would* try to change her," said Martin Ziegler.

4

"Father," said Josephine Ziegler. "This is Philip Stanley. Philip, my father."

"How do you do, sir," said Philip.

"Glad to see you," said Martin Ziegler. "I'm sorry my wife isn't here to meet you, but she's in Austria."

"I've met Mrs. Ziegler," said Philip. "Met her in Scotland, briefly. Very much impressed with her shooting."

"Oh, you like to shoot? So do I. What else do you like to do?"

"Oh, I suppose the usual. Tennis. Golf."

"No cricket?"

"Yes, cricket, too. But I seldom mention that to an American. They think it's a silly game, until they try it, that is."

"You have me there, right on the button. I've always thought it was a silly game, and I've never tried it. Did you play rugger?"

"Oh, you know about rugger?"

"I know about it. I'm fond of all sports, to some extent. I played football in high school."

"Oh, did you really?"

TWO BY O'HARA

"And what else do you like? Other than sports."

"Other than sports? I play a little."

"Philip plays the piano beautifully," said Josephine, interpreting.

"Not beautifully, not even skillfully. But intensely."

"I played the cornet in the boys' band, back home."

"I never knew you played the cornet, Father," said Josephine.

"Your mother discouraged it. She wanted to keep peace with the neighbors. When we were first married our house was so close to the house next door that my wife could borrow a cup of sugar without going outside. Next-door-neighbor would just pass it from her kitchen to ours."

"My father wants you to understand that he's a self-made man."

"There's nothing onerous about that, I'm sure," said Philip.

"About being one, or about bragging about it."

"Well---neither, really, I suppose," said Philip.

"You're going to be here two weeks, I believe," said Martin Ziegler.

"Yes."

"And at the opportune moment you were going to have a talk with me. Well, can't we have it now, and all relax?"

Philip looked at Josephine, then at Martin. "Well, I think you've anticipated me, but I don't really see why not."

"As far as I'm concerned, I give my consent."

Philip looked again at Josephine.

"I told you," she said.

"Told him what?" said Martin Ziegler.

"That getting your consent was the easiest part," said Josephine.

"Yes, and that I'd be taken completely by surprise, which I must say is no exaggeration," said Philip.

5

The wedding at the villa was in the house itself, since there was no Protestant church on the island. The reception was held under several striped marquees. The wedding guests were an impressive show, in frock coats and dress uniforms, with even the women wearing orders and decorations. There were hundreds of guests, and after the bride's father had danced with her and returned to a table where Dorothy was seated, he said: "No royalty came, but who would know the difference?"

"Everyone here knows the difference," said Dorothy.

"You wouldn't have, ten years ago, so don't be a spoilsport. It's a beautiful wedding, a beautiful bride, a fine day, and I like Philip Stanley. He'll be all right."

"If you let him."

"Now what do you mean by that?"

"Where are they going to live?"

"In England, of course. And visit here as often as they want to."

"Exactly," said Dorothy Ziegler.

"You're as wrong about that as you've been about various other things. For instance, you said I wouldn't like Philip. I do."

"Nothing will convince me of that. But you convinced him, and you even convinced Josephine. But not me. Oh, you've become quite an expert at manipulating people's lives. If you had opposed this marriage, you'd have lost Josephine and she'd have married him anyway. This way---well, there comes a time in every marriage when things look bad. When that happens to Josephine, she'll come back, and without Philip."

"If that's what you believe, why didn't you warn her?"

"I tried."

"Oh, you did, did you? And you got nowhere."

"Obviously."

"Do you know why you got nowhere, Dorothy?"

TWO BY O'HARA

"Tell me. I'm dying to know," she said wearily.

"Because she's so much like you."

"What?"

"Yes. And you don't like yourself. Josephine *is* like you but what she sees she doesn't admire."

"Nonsense," said Dorothy, but plainly she was admitting to herself the truth of what he was saying.

"Oh, yes. She is like you, but she doesn't want to be what you've become."

"And what is that?" she said, defiantly.

"Well, for instance," said Martin Ziegler. He rose to greet the Count Von Lemnitzer. "My dear Count Von Lemnitzer," he said. "Dorothy and I are so pleased that you could come." Von Lemnitzer, tall, thin, humorless, was nearing the end of his affair with Dorothy Ziegler, and they both knew it. The count was going through the experience of returning his mistress to her husband, but in this case the husband was not making it easy for him. Martin Ziegler was not overjoyed to get his wife back, which would have left the count feeling like a gracious person; nor was Ziegler apparently holding a grudge. Ziegler's behavior made the affair seem, retroactively, unimportant and cheap, and the unimportance and cheapness now rubbed off on the Austrian.

"I am so pleased to be able to come," said the count. "You were so kint to inwite me."

"Not a bit. All Europe seems to be here," said Martin, and the count sensed the implied snub. "Will you excuse me, you two? My old friend Paul Giraud."

Grinning to himself, Martin made his way to Paul Giraud, the former employee who had helped him six years earlier. "Aren't you glad I let you go six years ago? I hear you've prospered."

"A little bit," said Paul. "But who is to say I would not have prospered with you, Martin? Look." He indicated the fashionable crowd, the conspicuous spending of money.

The Man Who Could Not Lose

"This is how it turned out. It might have been very different. How many ships do you own now?"

"We have ten ships, but four of them are very small and none of them is very large."

"It's a beginning, Paul. Who is that dancing with my daughter?"

"Don't you know?"

"There are a lot of people I don't know."

"But that is someone you ought to know. His father is Lord Bedlington."

"And his father is a crook. Do you know the son?"

"Only by reputation."

"The way you say it, the reputation is not good."

"It is very bad."

"How does the son of a man like Bedlington get a bad reputation?"

"How does anyone? Money, and women."

"Oh, the same way his father did. Pardon me for saying so, Paul, but I wish I could look around and find one decent American."

Paul smiled ironically. "I wish I could look around and find one decent European."

Martin Ziegler laughed. "Well, there's you."

"And there's you, too, Martin. But what is it you say? I have cut some corners, too."

"Well, then, as one scoundrel to another, let's have a glass of champagne." He took two filled glasses off the tray carried by a passing waiter. "Here's to crime."

"Here's to crime unpunished."

"Is it ever?" said Martin Ziegler, suddenly serious.

Paul shrugged his shoulders. "So far."

TWO BY O'HARA

6

A year passed, and Martin Ziegler was sitting in his library, clasping and unclasping his hands. Brooks, his secretary, was looking out the window. "May I ask what you expect to see, looking out that window?" said Martin Ziegler.

"I've no idea, sir. I did notice that the wind is shifting. We're due for a bit of weather."

A Frenchman with a spade beard interrupted them. "My congratulations, sir."

"I have a grandson?" said Martin Ziegler.

"A granddaughter. X kilos."

"How is my daughter?"

"Your daughter is asleep, but she is well. That is, she will be well, I feel sure."

"You feel *sure*. You mean you have some doubts?"

"I feel sure she will be well. I shall remain here for a few days."

"You're damn right you will," said Martin. "You'll remain here till she *is* well."

The doctor ignored the threat. "You may see the child, if you wish."

A nurse brought the child to Martin Ziegler, who looked at it with little interest.

"Please to hold the child," said the doctor.

"Must I?"

"It is your grandchild," said the doctor. "You are the grandfather. The father is not here, the grandmothers are not here. The mother is asleep. Will you welcome this child into the world, or will you wait until God gives you what you want, a grandson? Make no mistake, Mr. Ziegler, a newborn child needs someone to welcome it."

"Oh, come on, Doctor."

"Then *I* shall hold the child," said the doctor. In French he said

The Man Who Could Not Lose

to the nurse: "Give me the infant," and held out his arms. But Martin Ziegler stepped in and took the baby in his arms. He looked at it and then looked at the doctor. "Is this what you want me to do? Is this welcoming the baby?"

"When the mother was born did you want a son?"

"Of course."

"And did you show your disappointment?"

"I don't remember. Yes, I guess I did."

"Yes," said the doctor. "And continued to show your disappointment for many years. And then tried to make up for your stupidity."

"Who told you that?"

"You did. The kind of man you are, sir. The kind of man who would threaten a physician. Who must have things his way. I have no fear of you, Mr. Ziegler."

"Obviously," dividing his attention between the baby in his arms and the doctor.

"I shall remain here precisely until I am ready to leave, but no longer. Kindly remember that, Mr. Ziegler. And remember it all your life."

"I could use a man like you," said Martin Ziegler.

"I could use a man like you---in my lectures. I am an anthropologist as well as an obstetrician."

"I like you."

"Too bad, Mr. Ziegler, because I---don't---like---you." The doctor left, while Brooks and the nurse stood and watched the new grandfather slowly succumbing to the charm of the infant.

7

A week or so later Josephine Ziegler Stanley and her father were sitting on the terrace. Within sight was the nurse, pushing the baby's pram. "I've had a letter from Sir John Caster. Your divorce is proceeding without difficulty."

"What about your own divorce, Father?"

"It is not proceeding."

"Why not? If Mother wants a divorce, why don't you give it to her? You were willing enough in my case."

"That's different. You're young and can get a new start in life. Your mother is not young. She'll only make a fool of herself. Not that she hasn't already."

"Well, let her. It's her life."

"Not entirely. It's partly mine."

"How so?"

"In many ways. She can't have a divorce for the asking, you know. The marriage didn't turn out well, but now that it hasn't I'm making the best of it."

"The only way you're making the best of it is that staying married protects you from designing females."

"That's exactly right. I'm certainly not holding on to your mother in any hope that she and I will ever make a go of it again. But I once owned some stock in a gold mine. Turned out there wasn't enough gold to cap a set of teeth. But I held on to it, and I've made over two million dollars out of it. Not from gold. From copper. Oh, I've made some bad investments, but I sure hate to lose, and I don't give up very easily. And I've made investments that looked pretty foolish, but I knew what I was doing. Once I bought a bankrupt railway. 'Ziegler, you're losing your mind,' they said. But I made a profit. Sold the property to two western states that used the roadbed for a highway."

"You might want to marry again."

The Man Who Could Not Lose

"I *have* wanted to, on one or two occasions. But that's where your mother's been such a great help, unintentionally. That's why I put up with her extravagances. In the long run they save me money, and they protect my independence."

"Will you answer something truthfully?"

"I usually do, with you."

"Did you let Mother know that my baby was coming early?"

He paused. "No, I didn't."

"I'm glad you admitted it. I knew you hadn't."

"How did you know, Josephine? And why did you try to trap me? Don't do that."

"I had a letter from Mother. She's coming home next week, to be here when the baby is born."

"Then there's no damage done, is there? We were spared her fussing around."

"I wish she had been here. I just wish she'd been here."

"Do you hold it against me that she wasn't?"

"I would have, if I hadn't seen how much you love the baby. You do love my baby, don't you?"

"From the moment I set eyes on her," he said. He leaned forward and looked out over the sea. "And I'm glad you had a daughter."

"You are, honestly? Not a grandson?"

He pointed out to sea. "Look out there. Do you see those destroyers?"

"Yes."

"Do you know who they belong to?"

"I can't see the flags."

"You don't need to. They belong to Mr. Mussolini. Mr. Mussolini and I you might say arrived at the same time. He led his boys into Rome, and I smuggled my little family to this island. That was 1922. He has great plans, Mussolini. But a lot of sons are going to be killed dead if his plans go through."

"Whose sons? Not Americans."

TWO BY O'HARA

"You're not an American, my girl. You're British, and so is your daughter, and so would your son be if you'd had a son."

"Are the British sons going to be killed?"

"I don't see how it can be avoided," said Martin Ziegler. "Mussolini told me---"

"Mussolini told *you?*"

"Why, yes. I'm in touch with Mussolini."

"You are? Do you know him?"

"I've never met him, face to face, but---Josephine, don't you know that your father's a big man? I'm a big man, girl."

"I knew you were awfully rich, but. . . ."

"Listen, the kind of rich I am now, people like Mussolini have to do business with people like me."

"Are you a supporter of Mussolini?"

"Loosely speaking, I suppose you might say I am." He studied her face. "He sent you a wedding present."

"Oh, I know he did. A perfectly beautiful Venetian chest, mahogany. But I thought that was because Philip's uncle was something in the British Foreign Office."

"Like hell it was. Philip's uncle? Philip's uncle is pretty far down in the scheme of things. I'd be very much surprised if Mussolini ever heard of him. Have you been thinking all this time that all those generals and ambassadors came to the wedding because it was Philip's wedding?"

"Yes."

"And those wedding presents from kings and prime ministers?"

"Yes."

"Who do you think those men are that come and go all the time?"

"Businessmen?"

"Indeed they are. They're the men who advise governments, and *I* advise *them.* Why do you think I have a wireless station on 24-hour duty? Why do you think so many of my visitors arrive in

The Man Who Could Not Lose

battleships and seaplanes? You've never been to the hotel down in the village. It's a funny place. It's full of people who are spying on each other and keeping tabs on every visitor to the island. There's a bridge game been going on for three years, and all four of the players are spies from different European countries. Do you know that Brooks is a spy? Of course you don't, and I'm not supposed to, but I've known it ever since I hired him. He's a British spy, and a week after he came the Italians told me who he was."

"Then why do you keep him?"

"Because anybody I get to take his place will be a spy. Naturally the Italians would like to have their own man in Brooks's job, and so would the French and Germans. But I'm used to Brooks, so I keep him. And of course he may be spying for the Germans now. Brooks knows that I know he's a spy, although we never discuss it."

"He doesn't look like the kind of man who'd be a spy."

"Neither does your baby's nurse."

"Pauline? No!"

"Of course she is. I shouldn't really call them spies. They're agents. They find out what they can, what little they can, and report back to their governments. They don't steal plans. I have no maps or anything like that. Most of it is up here," he said, tapping his head.

"What exactly do you do?"

"Well, I'm a sort of clearing-house of financial information. Some of it comes over the wireless, some of it I get from the men who visit me, some by mail from Paris, London, Berlin, New York and Washington, Basle, Rome, and so on. I assess the information, and then I decide what to do with it. You see, I'm here on this rather remote island and I'm not influenced by the men around me, the way I would be if I operated in Paris or London or New York. My judgment is my own, and it's been pretty good."

"I know, but what do you do? Do you buy a stock and sell it at a profit?"

TWO BY O'HARA

"Oh, no. That was the kind of thing I used to do, when I was younger. No, I deal in exchange. It's called arbitrage. There are only about a dozen men in the world who really understand it, and I'm one of them. It's guessing how much the dollar is going to be worth in Paris tomorrow, or how much the franc is going to be worth in New York. But it's a lot more complicated than that. Out of a dozen men in the world who understand it, I put myself about Number 8. Number 1 is a Chinese gentleman. Then there are two Swiss gentlemen, two Frenchmen, two Englishmen, and one American. I guess I'm Number 9. But I'm the only one that hasn't got a government behind him, and that's why I'm important. My judgment is not influenced by patriotism or politics."

"Father, how much are you worth?"

"How much do you think is a lot?"

"Oh---a hundred million pounds."

He smiled. "If you'd said dollars instead of pounds I could have stuck out my chest."

"You have that many dollars?"

"Yes, and more. But it could all go in a week's time, if I didn't keep my eyes and ears open. And it's not dollars. I'm out of dollars. There's going to be a panic in New York. Now don't you repeat that. If Brooks heard me say that it would be very valuable information, coming from me. If Philip Stanley's uncle knew I said it he'd make millions on it."

"Are you going to make millions on it?"

"Yes."

"And you're just waiting?"

"Yes." A servant appeared with a message from the wireless station. Martin Ziegler read the message. "I didn't have long to wait," he said.

The Man Who Could Not Lose

8

"I consider what you did inexcusable," said Dorothy Ziegler.

"I don't remember asking you to excuse me," said Martin Ziegler. "I didn't want you around when the baby was born."

"I had as much right to be here as you."

"But I don't think so. You've been traipsing around Europe while Josephine was growing up. You got her into a bad marriage with a second-rate Englishman, a nincompoop."

"If you felt that way you could have stopped the marriage."

"Oh, no. I could have stopped the marriage, *maybe*, but I'd have lost Josephine."

"Yes, that was your plan," said Dorothy. "And now she's back, without a husband, and the baby without a father."

"It could be much worse."

"I don't see how," said Dorothy.

"Then I'll tell you. You could make it worse by hanging around here."

"Why? Have you other plans for Josephine?"

"I have great plans for Josephine and the baby."

"I suppose it would be foolish to ask what they are," said Dorothy.

"It would be. Not that you're above doing foolish things. So *many* foolish things, Dorothy. And *doing* them so foolishly. When are you leaving?"

"I've just got here."

"That doesn't answer my question."

"I want to be with my daughter's child."

He laughed. "What's the matter, Dorothy? Are you afraid to say grandchild? Doesn't this new fellow know you're a grandma?"

"If he doesn't, I suppose you'll manage to see that he does."

"Well, that wouldn't be too difficult. He's waiting for you less than fifty miles from here."

TWO BY O'HARA

"Oh, you're so thorough, Martin."

"Yes, even in little things like that. So when are you returning to your languishing lover?"

"Why is it so important for me to leave so soon?"

"If you thought a minute you'd be able to guess."

"Well, if it isn't Mrs. Raleigh, then it must be someone you've picked out for Josephine."

"You're pretty thorough, too."

"Not at all. Mrs. Raleigh makes no secret of your interest in her. It gets her in a lot of places that had stopped welcoming her. Not to mention what it does *for* her credit. I said for her credit, not *to* her credit."

"Yes, you and Mrs. Raleigh have a lot in common. When I compare the bills I think you two must be having a competition."

"Who's ahead, Martin?"

"Naturally you are, Dorothy. As my wife, you have the edge. Of course you wouldn't have that edge if you stopped being my wife."

"Then you're not going to give me a divorce?"

"It's a tiresome subject. Why bring it up again? No."

"Have you ever stopped to think what you're doing to Josephine? Do you think it does a young girl much good to watch her father destroying her mother?"

"Am I destroying you, Dorothy?"

"I still have sense enough to see that. Yes. But it isn't what you're doing to me. Erik Von Lemnitzer wanted to marry me, but now he's gone. There's someone else, waiting in Juan-les-Pins. And there'll more than likely be others. But what you don't see is the terrible thing you're doing to Josephine."

"What terrible thing is that? Enlighten me."

"Some day she's going to realize that you destroyed her almost the same way you did me. And the cruelest thing is that she's going to blame herself for failing to heed the warning, the warning that was in what you've done to me."

"She doesn't consider it a warning."

The Man Who Could Not Lose

"Naturally. But let me ask you this. What has Josephine ever done to you?"

"Done to me?"

"I made a big mistake, and so you're getting your revenge. Frank Blackwell made another mistake, and you've had your revenge on him. I suppose you know he committed suicide."

"I couldn't have stopped that."

"Oh, yes you could. You owed him money."

"No I didn't. I paid him what I owed him long ago."

"Then I'm sorry. I thought you owed him a lot."

"Not a penny."

"But he was penniless."

"He took the money I gave him and paid some of the other people I did owe. That was none of his business."

"Ah, now I see. He went broke paying your debts."

"He went broke meddling in my affairs. But that has nothing to do with Josephine."

"Oh, hasn't it? She's your daughter, therefore you can ruin her without any excuse at all. It doesn't have to be revenge."

"And what I do for Josephine doesn't have to be destructive, either. That's your interpretation of it. A rejected wife and a rejected mother. Josephine made her mistake, with a lot of help from you. The next time she'll be wiser."

"With a man you've picked out, no doubt."

"Yes."

"Although she's still in love with Philip. Just as I stayed in love with you. But you're an unforgiving bastard."

"I took my loss, as far as you were concerned."

"Oh, sure. And turned your loss into a profit, as usual. Poor Mrs. Raleigh. Poor Josephine. And God help my grandchild." She was suddenly weak and beaten.

"Grandchild, eh? It cost you quite an effort to say that word."

"It costs me an effort to go on living."

9

"This," said Martin Ziegler, "is General Paladino. Dino, my daughter Josephine."

Paladino, exquisitely tailored, brown from the sun, slender, tall, and with the look of concern or preoccupation that is characteristic of so many Italian aristocrats, was in his middle thirties.

"You've heard of the general," said Martin Ziegler.

"Yes, I have," said Josephine.

"But we're not going to mention aviation. The general is here for a well-earned rest, and we're going to pretend that no such person as Leonardo da Vinci ever existed."

"Why do you say da Vinci, Martin?"

"Well, didn't he invent the flying machine?"

"You are priceless! I shall enjoy my visit with your father, Mrs. Stanley. He is a stimulating man."

"Not too stimulating, I hope. You're here to relax. If you want to play tennis, you'll have to ask Josephine. I was never a tennis player. But I'll swim with you twice a day, and we have two or three pretty good horses, if you'd like to ride. Josephine is a good rider."

In the next two weeks Martin Ziegler stayed in the background, while Paladino and Josephine were maneuvered into a romance. After the first few days they were alone together at every frequent opportunity; sailing, riding, swimming in the surf, away from Martin Ziegler. At the end of his visit Paladino said goodbye to Martin at the villa, and Josephine drove him to the village and the pier, where he boarded a launch to take him to a seaplane.

"I think we did him a lot of good," said Martin. "He was much more relaxed when he left."

"You can relax, too," said Josephine.

"Why?" said Martin.

"It worked. I think I am in love with him."

"Then why should I relax? I certainly didn't intend---"

The Man Who Could Not Lose

"Stop pretending. It may not have been obvious to him, but it was to me. Well, it worked."

"Okay. You liked him, eh?"

"Can you imagine not liking him?"

"No, I can't. But I don't know about women," said Martin. "I like him because he's one of the few men that is so good at his job that he can speak up to Mussolini. I respect independence and ability. It's nice that he's a handsome dog and a good athlete and has great charm. But with Dino it doesn't end there."

"As it did with Philip, you're trying to say."

"He has all the good things Philip had, that a young girl would be impressed by. But a woman ought to look for other things."

"Well, he has them, and I saw them."

"The only thing I don't know is why he never got married."

"I do. He wouldn't give up flying when the girl he was in love with asked him to."

"How do you feel about that?"

"I feel the same way she did, but I wouldn't ask him to stop doing the thing he cares about most."

"Are you going to marry him?"

"I'm not going to let anything stop me."

Martin Ziegler grinned. "Just let anything try!" He kissed his daughter.

"You didn't *do* that when I got engaged to Philip."

"But this time I did. I'm rather proud of this."

"Don't say that, Father," she said, with some alarm. "I know what you did, but I'd rather think it was just Dino and I."

10

"Good evening, Mrs. Ziegler," said Philip Stanley. He was in a dinner jacket, she in an evening dress, and they were part of the crowd at a hotel in Switzerland, and both were dancing with other people. "Are you stopping here?"

"Yes, Philip dear. Lunch with me tomorrow."

"Delighted," said Philip Stanley.

They met for lunch. "You will want to know about my daughter," said Dorothy Ziegler.

"Not at all, but I should like to know about mine."

"You've never seen your daughter?"

"Never. I've tried, but I run up against a stone wall. A stone wall called Martin Ziegler."

"I know that stone wall. I've been on both sides of it."

"Presently on the side I'm on, if I may say so, and if what I hear is correct."

"It's no secret. You know, of course, that Josephine is married again."

"I've even written to her new husband, and he put up no strenuous objection to my seeing the child. But every time arrangements were made, they were cancelled---"

"At the last minute, of course."

"Always at the last minute."

"You musn't blame Josephine."

"I'm not wasting my time blaming anyone. I merely would like to see my daughter. Is that asking too much?"

"Yes, much too ·much. Her grandfather---maternal grand-father---is determined that the child will grow up without ever knowing you."

"So far, very successfully. I have a daughter over a year old, and I've never been permitted to see her. But I'm very persistent, Mrs. Ziegler."

The Man Who Could Not Lose

"Be careful."

"Is that a warning?"

"Yes."

"But I was given visiting privileges in the divorce."

"But first the child has to be in England, and that isn't going to happen. Philip, you don't love the child, so take my advice and pretend she doesn't exist. Don't try to see her. Because then it will happen. You will love her. She's adorable. And from then on it will be nothing but trouble. Believe me, I know."

"I don't see things that way. I am the father, and I want to see my child. I wouldn't think much of myself if I were to pretend she doesn't exist, and it makes me angry to be cheated out of seeing her. I'll go on trying, in spite of Mr. Ziegler."

"You won't win."

"We'll see."

"You'll see? Look at me. What else do you need to convince you. I'm forbidden to see my daughter *and* my granddaughter, and I'm not even divorced."

"Perhaps we could help each other."

"Don't count on me, Philip."

"Ah, but I do count on you."

11

"Your mother is in Switzerland with Philip Stanley."

"I can hardly believe that, Father."

Martin Ziegler handed her the telephone. "Call them yourself, either one. They're both at the San Remo in Davos."

"Hundreds of people are there now."

"Josephine, the only reason I keep tabs on who your mother is seeing is because I have to know for business reasons. There are some people in some governments that would like to get at me through her. Otherwise, she can live her own life."

"Then why tell me?"

"Because the one place Libby is safe from them is here. I would like you to leave her here with me."

"Mother wouldn't do that."

"Alone, maybe not. But she and Philip together might. If I were you, I'd keep her at her distance. Don't answer the telephone, don't answer letters. And let Libby stay here till that romance collapses, if it is a romance, and I'm not saying it is. However, I'm not saying it isn't."

12

"She won't even speak to me on the telephone," said Dorothy Ziegler.

"Then we'll have to do something else," said Philip.

13

"I am sorry, Mr. Stanley, but there is nothing I can do," said Paladino. "If Josephine does not wish to see you, you will surely be a gentleman. Please to stay away from this house."

14

"Philip, my boy," said Harold Stanley. "I appreciate the difficulties of the situation. Paternal love and so on. And there's a lot on your side. But does this child mean so much to you? You've never even seen the child in nearly two years' time."

"As things are going I may never see her."

"Yes. Hmm. But I wish I could persuade you to be patient, at least for the present. You *are* a British subject, and these encounters with the Italian police. Complaints by General Paladino, who is one of the few Fascisti that doesn't foam at the mouth at the mention of our country. . . ."

15

Philip Stanley, dejected and trying not to show it, sat beside Dorothy Ziegler and looked at the palms of his hands. "I seem to have lost, Dorothy. Even my own government. . . ."

She reached out a hand and put it on his shoulder. He suddenly turned to her, and they embraced. "He was hoping this would happen," she said.

"Then let it, shall we?"

She nodded and kissed him.

16

The very blonde girl said: "He was never anything but wonderful to me, whatever else he was. And I know the other things about him. But I was with him most of the time till I was twelve years old, and then I was sent to school in Switzerland. My mother was with her husband in Rome, and she had two children by Dino. They were all nice to me. Dino was lovely to me, and my mother was too. But my grandfather was my favorite, and I thought of the island as home and Grandfather as my real parent. Living that way, on the island all the time, I saw more of him than most girls do of their fathers, and I don't remember ever missing my real father. Grandfather was there to tell me stories about the United States--- where of course I'd never been. He taught me to swim and to ride, and we'd play cards together."

"Didn't you see any children your own age?"

"Oh, yes. The island doctor had a large family, and the mayor of the village. The lawyer's children. The man who owned the fishing fleet. The village banker. And my grandfather must have had fifty servants on the place, counting gardeners, and the wireless operators, and the housekeeper. Today you'd say that my playmates were carefully screened, but I didn't know that at the time. I did know that I was treated with deference by older people, but of course any child would know why. My grandfather was richer than anyone else on the island. We had the biggest house and the most ground and so on, and I was part of that."

"Weren't you ever curious about your real father?"

"Not very. I'd never seen him, and children, if they're brought up in a certain way and never know any other way, they accept that."

"But didn't you *ask* about your father?"

"Yes," said the girl. "Once. And my grandfather told me he was dead."

"And you believed him?"

The Man Who Could Not Lose

"No, because I knew he was alive. But I had been told a lie by my grandfather, the only time I didn't like him. I was nine or ten, I guess. Old enough to be upset when I caught him in a lie. And I never asked him any more. I couldn't bear to have him lie to me. He was so perfect otherwise."

"What about your grandmother?"

"She only appeared once while I was there."

17

"Why have you come here? There is no excuse for this," said Martin Ziegler.

"Must I have an excuse?" said Dorothy Ziegler.

"More than an excuse. My permission, and I've refused you that a hundred times. I don't want you around, especially when Libby is staying with me."

"That's why I came, because I heard she was here."

"You're not going to see her. You're not spending one night here. You got in this time, because the servants didn't know any better. The next time you won't get past the gate. Where is Philip Stanley? If your skirts were longer he'd be hiding behind them, I suppose."

"Where is Mrs. Raleigh? I didn't ask you that."

"Mrs. Raleigh is a thing of the past. You're not as well informed as you used to be."

"Oh, who is it now?"

"Snoop a little. You have nothing better to do."

"I hear her. Is that Libby?"

They could hear the little girl's voice from the hall. "Yes it is, but if you give any sign of who you are, I'll stop your money forever. You know I mean that."

The girl Libby, followed by the governess, entered the room. The governess recognized Dorothy Ziegler, but kept a frozen face. "Grandfather, I took a spill and I didn't cry," said the child. Then she looked frankly, with cool curiosity, at Dorothy, who gave no sign, and in so doing gave the child an impression of aloofness. The child made a perfunctory curtsey.

"I can see you did," said Martin Ziegler. "You skun your kneecap. And you didn't cry? Good girl. I'll see you in a little while."

The governess and child left, and there were tears in Dorothy's eyes. "I'll leave," she said.

"You behaved very well."

"How dare you say that to me? I was afraid to defy you, but I don't have to accept your approval."

"Just my way of telling you you passed the test. The money continues, and isn't that all that matters?"

"Until even that doesn't matter. Then---"

"Then you'll be dangerous. I know that." He filled and lit a pipe. "Would your friend Philip like to *earn* some money, for a change?"

"Not your money."

"Why don't you ask him? I give you enough for two, but he might like to have some of his own. Unless, of course, that's the only hold you have on him. If that's the case, I withdraw my offer."

"What do you want?"

"The thought occurred to me that the last person people would suspect of acting in my behalf is Philip Stanley. I want to know something. He could probably find it out, and if he does I'll pay him well. Isn't he at the hotel right this minute? Call him. Tell him I want to see him."

The Man Who Could Not Lose

The call was made and in a few minutes Philip Stanley appeared.

"Ah, there you are," said Martin Ziegler. "We won't waste any time in politeness. The smell of money brought you here, so down to business. You have an uncle in the Foreign Office. I want to know whether the French are going to let Italy have equal status with the United States, Britain, and Japan and themselves in this new naval treaty. I will pay you 5,000 pounds for the information if delivered in two weeks. And if the information proves to be correct, another 10,000 pounds later. Are you agreeable?"

"What do you think I am?"

"This is information. You're not selling out your country. You're not being a traitor. Your country is not involved. It's what the French are going to do about the Italians that I want to know."

"My uncle wouldn't give me that information even if he had it."

"He doesn't have to know he's giving it, if you're casual enough about asking him. And he does have the information. Also, I think he has it right. That's $75,000 for one casual conversation. A man can live very comfortably on that for five years."

"Don't do it, Philip," said Dorothy.

"Of course I won't do it," said Philip.

"The money will be paid in pounds, dollars, marks, yen, any way you like, and in cash. You don't have to let *her* know you're doing it. I'm sure she keeps some things from you."

"You see what he's doing, Philip? He's destroying us."

"Jolly well wasting his time, too," said Philip.

"A man could buy a schooner and sail around the world, a man with $75,000 cash."

"Let's get out of here, Dorothy."

18

A week later Philip Stanley appeared at the villa. "I have the information."

"How do you want the money?"

"I want it equally divided in pounds, dollars, and francs."

"And when the information is confirmed, a couple of months from now? Where shall I send that money?"

"To Hong Kong. I'll give you the name of my bank there."

"Here is your money," said Martin, taking it from a wall safe. "Pounds, dollars, and francs, at this morning's rate of exchange. Sterling."

Philip picked up the notes and put them in a case which he returned to his coat pocket. "The French are going to oppose letting the Italians in on an equal footing with the other nations," he said.

"Do you know how they're going to do it?"

"That information wasn't part of the bargain."

"No, it wasn't, but I thought I'd get a little extra."

"You get precisely what you asked for and no more. I got that much without arousing suspicion, and I didn't ask any more questions."

"Fine. And you're off to Hong Kong?"

"I sail from Marseilles day after tomorrow."

"You will hear from me. That is, your bank will be notified. Good day, sir."

"You're sure England won't be involved. I have no reason to trust you, but I do."

"You have no reason to trust me, and you'll be paid in full. Now if you don't mind, I'm a busy man."

Suddenly the horror of what he had done came over Philip Stanley, and he left.

19

The schooner put out to sea with one man, Philip Stanley, aboard. He stopped the motor and hoisted sail. He stood grim-faced at the wheel and there was no sound but the sound of the breeze in the sheets. Then there was the sound of a single pistol shot, and the yacht, with no control at the wheel, began to make crazy figures on the water.

20

"Il Duce asked me to give you this," said Dino. He held open a leather box in which lay a medal and ribbon to be worn about the neck. "He said you would know what it is for."

"Well, now, he didn't have to do that. And when would I ever wear a medal?" said Martin Ziegler.

"It is the highest decoration he gives."

"It is?"

"And he must think you earned it. A lot of men would give a great deal to have that decoration. For myself, I am very happy that you would do something of such importance for my country, even if I don't know what it is you did."

Josephine smiled at her husband and at her father. "Can't you give us a hint, Father?"

"Well, now---a hint?" Martin considered. "No, I can only say that I followed my lifelong custom of turning a loss into a profit."

21

Brooks and Martin Ziegler were in the villa office, at work. Martin Ziegler looked up from his desk and saw Dorothy Ziegler standing in the doorway. She was staring at her husband with cold, intense malevolence. "I thought I told you---" he began, but remembering the presence of Brooks he checked himself. "Brooks, come back later."

Brooks rose, bowed and spoke to Dorothy on his way out, but she ignored him. He closed the door behind him, but he stood outside and listened.

"You killed Philip," she said.

"I was under the impression that he killed himself. There was no one else on the boat with him, not even you. A lucky thing for you, too, because you might have been suspected."

"Yes, you saw to that. You corrupted him, you bribed him to leave me, and you made him realize what he had done to his country." She took a pistol out of her bag and aimed it at Martin Ziegler. Her first shot struck the woodwork behind him, the second struck his hand, which he had raised in a now-wait gesture. He was thrown back by the impact of the bullet, and she turned the pistol on herself, but he got to her before she could pull the trigger and snatched it from her. Brooks rushed in.

"This went off in my hand," said Martin Ziegler. "Look what I did to myself. *Do you see, Brooks?* I shot myself *in the hand*, and the other bullet must be back there somewhere. Mrs. Ziegler is badly frightened. I guess she thought I killed myself."

Dorothy had fainted.

"'She'll be all right," said Ziegler.

"But I must get the doctor for you, sir."

"First let's put her on the sofa," said Ziegler. As they did so he said to Brooks: "Lucky, wasn't it, that you hadn't gone very far?"

"I was standing just outside the door," said Brooks.

The Man Who Could Not Lose

"I had a feeling you would be," said Ziegler. "I often have that feeling, Brooks. You've become very valuable to me, you know."

"Have I indeed, sir? Here, let me wrap a tourniquet about that wrist."

"And not as just a first-aid man."

"Oh, I understand, Mr. Ziegler."

"I'm sure you do. In fact, I often wish that I could have your services exclusively."

"Do you, sir?"

"But patriotism comes first, naturally."

"Does it, necessarily? You remember what Voltaire said, that patriotism is the last refuge of the scoundrel?"*

"I do remember that. The last refuge of the scoundrel. So perhaps it doesn't come first."

"Not for scoundrels, Mr. Ziegler. There we are. Now let me call Dr. LeGrande."

"Before you do, Brooks, would you mind making sure that you have everything straight in your mind?"

"Oh, I'm sure. Weren't you suggesting that Mrs. Ziegler with all that jewelry, and traveling alone so much, ought to have a pistol? And the thing went off in your hand."

"Why, yes, Brooks. You could hear every word we said, couldn't you?"

"Voices carry in these old houses."

"They do, don't they? Mrs. Ziegler is coming to. Why don't you make your call in another room. I want to reassure her when she recovers consciousness."

"Yes, you reassure her, sir," said Brooks, leaving.

"I heard everything you said, both of you," said Dorothy.

"Did you? The question is, Dorothy, what to do about you?"

"Have me killed."

*Samuel Johnson was responsible for this epigram.

TWO BY O'HARA

"Well, that isn't entirely up to me. I may be able to keep Brooks quiet, although he knows now---thanks to you---that Philip's suicide wasn't over a love affair. But keeping you quiet is another matter, and as I say, not entirely up to me. My friend in Rome wouldn't like you to go to the British Foreign Office. And if you did, it would mean the end of Philip's uncle, so you'd have that on your conscience. And don't forget that your daughter is married to an Italian general. But rather than have you go to the British, I think my friend in Rome would manage to have *something* happen to you. It wouldn't be difficult, either. What more natural than for you to commit suicide after your lover did? You see what I mean? . . . If your aim had been better I wouldn't be worrying about any of these things."

"There's something else, too, Martin."

"What?"

"Your own position. If I did go to the British Foreign Office, all Europe would find out that you were working with Mussolini."

"Yes. All Europe. That would certainly curtail some of my activities."

"This is a French island, and the French wouldn't like it at all."

"I'm sure they wouldn't. I think you'd better stay here for a while."

"Is that what you've decided?"

"Yes. You came here to effect a reconciliation, and I was willing. That's reasonable, isn't it?"

"And what happens to me?"

"Well, Dorothy, you came here to kill me. That's about as far as you can go, isn't it?"

"I could run away."

"You wouldn't get past the gate."

"Then I'm a prisoner?"

"You're a live prisoner."

"For how long?"

The Man Who Could Not Lose

"Until this whole damn thing becomes unimportant. After that you can go anywhere and say whatever you please. Things are moving faster all the time."

She laughed sardonically. "And I came here to kill you."

He smiled in triumph. "You drew blood. This hurts, too."

22

The two Italians with their attache cases seated themselves, declined drinks, lit cigarettes, and waited for Martin Ziegler to open the meeting.

"Gentlemen, some time ago you kindly informed me that the man you just saw, Brooks, my secretary, is a British agent. It's about him I wish to speak to you, and why I asked you to come immediately. Yesterday there was an unfortunate accident in this room. My wife came here to shoot me, and did. But the dangerous part of the whole thing is that Brooks overheard more than he should have." Ziegler went on to relate the circumstances of Dorothy, Philip Stanley, and her desire to avenge Philip. "And so I wanted you to get here before Brooks could start talking. I have been tempting him with money, and he's holding out for a very large sum. I told him I'd let him know tomorrow. That gave me a little time. Have you any suggestions as to the future of Mr. Brooks?"

"Speaking for myself, Mr. Ziegler, I would almost predict that Mr. Brooks has no future," said the older Italian.

"And I concur," said the younger. "What are his habits? His pastimes?"

Ziegler smiled. "In the afternoon, when I take my nap, he takes

his binoculars and goes bird-watching. On the other side of the island there are some steep cliffs where I believe certain unusual specimens are to be seen. Of course I never know when he's going there."

"He could be taken there," said the younger Italian.

"Or invited. I know something of birds, and if I express the wish to see those on the other side of the island. . . ."

23

The gendarmes laid a pair of binoculars on Martin Ziegler's desk. "Do you recognize these, Mr. Ziegler?"

Martin Ziegler picked them up and examined them. "Well, I've seen many like them. Wait a minute. G. F. R. B. Those are my secretary's initials. These must belong to him. Where did you get them?"

"Beside the body of a man who was at the bottom of the cliffs."

"What was the man wearing?"

"Grey trousers, white shirt, blue sweater, and tennis shoes."

"Brooks!" said Martin Ziegler. "That's what he was wearing when I went up to take my nap last Tuesday afternoon. You said the body. Then he must be dead?"

"He has been dead since Tuesday, Mr. Ziegler."

"I must notify his family. And yet I don't know if he had any family. I really knew very little about him outside his work."

"Did he have any enemies that you know of?"

"On the theory that he might have been killed? I don't know. He had an annoying manner, supercilious, you might call it. But you know the English. They can be irritating without meaning to be."

The Man Who Could Not Lose

"Ah, yes, the English," said one gendarme, and the other nodded.

"Did he leave here alone?" said one of them. "And at what time?"

"I couldn't tell you. When he went bird-watching it was usually very early in the morning or in the afternoon while I was taking my nap."

"You had some visitors that day."

"I don't think so. Let me look on my calendar. Here. Yes Monday I had visitors, two Italian gentlemen. They stayed overnight and had lunch here Tuesday, and then I suppose they returned to Rome. Do you want their names? One is Professor Marlatti, the other is his assistant, a young man named Spolito, both in the Ministry of Finance. Neither of them knew Brooks. The next day I had two visitors from Switzerland. Dr. Schlegel and Dr. Zumbach, Swiss bankers. They also stayed overnight. In fact their visit was prolonged because Brooks was not here. He knew where certain papers were and I had to find them myself. I'm sorry to hear he met with an accident, but I must say his absence has caused me a great deal of inconvenience. He had his own system of filing papers, and he was very secretive."

"Secretive?" The gendarmes exchanged glances. "Did he ever have visitors?"

"Here? Of course not. I know that he used to meet friends at the hotel, but he wasn't permitted to have them here."

The gendarmes nodded to each other understandingly.

"You two are making him out to be a much more interesting man than I ever found him to be. He was very efficient, but very dull. Just what I wanted in a secretary."

"Be assured, Monsieur, he was not dull. Thank you very much. You have been very kind."

"Why is he now so interesting?"

They smiled politely and shook their heads.

24

The door to Martin's office was open, and Dorothy stood in the doorway. "May I come in?" she said.

"Sure, come on in. Have a cigarette. Put your feet up and relax."

"Such a hearty welcome. I didn't expect it."

"Well, what did you expect? If I surprised you, you've surprised me the past two months."

"Why?"

"Because you didn't cause any trouble. Not that you'd have got very far, but you've made things easier for everybody. What's on your mind?"

"I'd like to leave."

"Not yet."

"Hasn't the Brooks affair blown over?"

"Don't call it the Brooks affair, please, Dorothy. Somehow or other that creates a doubt that it was an accident."

"Yes it does, doesn't it?"

"Very much so, and I'd never want you to leave here if I thought you'd start wandering around Europe and speaking of it as l'affaire Brooks."

"I can see why you wouldn't."

"The press handled it correctly. Little squibs that said my secretary fell to his death on a bird-watching field trip. Then no more about it."

"The press can be so obliging at times."

"At times. Why do you want to leave here and start that useless life again? You look rested."

"And I am rested, God knows why."

"You look more than rested. The air, the sunshine, the quiet life---they've restored your good looks. Two months ago you came in here to shoot me, but quite frankly---well, maybe something has

The Man Who Could Not Lose

happened to us. I know it has to me. And we're two married people, Dorothy. We're not kids.''

"And you haven't appointed a successor to Mrs. Raleigh."

"No, I haven't. Why don't *you* succeed Mrs. Raleigh?"

"Because I was your wife."

"Technically, still are my wife. But I'm not asking you to consider me as your husband."

"What then?"

"Well, I could be a successor to Von Lemnitzer, and Stanley, and several others we don't have to mention. A new man in your life. And after all, I'm not the man you married. The ambitious farm boy from the wheat belt that played a cornet. And you're not the girl from New Rochelle, New York, that I eloped with. I couldn't have met the governor of Minnesota then, but now I get medals from kings and dictators. And you---well, you were listed as one of the best-dressed women in Europe last year, the only American in the whole bunch. If you were you, and I was me, the way we are now, and not two people that had been married to each other all those years, you and I would be almost certain to be getting together just about now."

"Yes, I never thought of us that way."

"The women I've known, such as Mrs. Raleigh, you're one of them now, Dorothy."

"And you're the kind of man they want. Rich and powerful and very realistic."

"Realistic comes first. I was realistic, then I became rich, then I became powerful."

"I suppose so. Meanwhile, you're suggesting that I become your mistress?"

"I am."

"I'm not ready to. I know that men who become as powerful as you---they have to be ruthless."

TWO BY O'HARA

"Realistic."

"And if I were just meeting you, I don't suppose I'd be too surprised to learn that three men had died on account of you."

"What three men?"

"Frank Blackwell. Philip Stanley, and Brooks, whose first name I never knew. I'm sure that other men like you have caused many more deaths. Wars and revolutions. Assassinations."

He was staring at her fiercely, and paid little attention to the latter part of her remarks. "Go on thinking what you like about Blackwell and Philip Stanley. But be careful what you say about Brooks."

"I guess I should. That really was murder, wasn't it? I'll be more careful about Brooks."

"I warned you, Dorothy. Keeping you quiet isn't entirely up to me. This conversation would make some people consider you a very dangerous woman. And there's nothing I could do to protect you."

"Even if you wanted to."

"All right, even if I wanted to. Bear this in mind, because I always do. I am powerful, because I am useful. But I could fall off a cliff, too." He stopped suddenly, aware that he had put too much into words.

She half smiled. "I have a feeling that your romantic notions have suddenly disappeared."

Now he smiled, but not from joviality. "Anything but," he said, and took her in his arms forcibly. She resisted, freed herself.

"Don't do that," she said, and hurried out of the room. He looked at the bullet wound scar on his hand and smiled.

25

From the very first day of his occupancy, Martin Ziegler's villa and the walled-in estate had been such a strange establishment, with such strange goings-on, that the island natives had come to accept unusual happenings as commonplace. Martin Ziegler's distribution of largesse and graft prevented inquisitiveness and trespassing and other such undesirable activity. Over the years, too, the islanders appreciated the fact that the man in the villa was a person of consequence among the great of Europe and that he enjoyed undefined rights and privileges such as a kind of extra-territoriality that made the happenings behind his walls immune to investigation. They had found out that he owned nearly everything on the island---the hotel, the bank, the fishing fleet--- and had taken over possession of these sources of income without any fuss and without interfering with the islanders' lives. But they knew their livelihood was always subject to decisions of Martin Ziegler. He had never invoked his power, but neither had any islander challenged it.

The islanders seldom saw him. His visits to the village were rare, and invariably were made by motor, in a carriage, or on horseback. But when he did appear in the village he was a pleasant-seeming man; jovial, careful to reply to those who greeted him, and in general exhibiting a manner that was calculated to allay any suspicions or fear. A fisherman who wanted to complain about the condition of his boat could speak to Martin Ziegler on the village street, and the complaint would be listened to, a note made of it, and the condition rectified. Any clerk or laborer could do the same, if he happened to catch Martin Ziegler on one of his visits to the village. The illusion thus was created that M. Ziegler was a generous, reasonable man, who would do what was right if he knew the facts. But no islander had any hope of passing through the gate in order to present his case. The lower class consequently

TWO BY O'HARA

believed that their immediate superiors were the real wall between themselves and M. Ziegler, which was what M. Ziegler wanted them to believe. The middle class knew and cared only that under M. Ziegler's patronage salaries went on without interruption, regardless of the catches made by the fishing fleet or the good or bad harvests in the island vineyards. Under these conditions the island and the islanders flourished and inevitably word of this continuing prosperity reached the mainland, with the result that many mainlanders sought to establish residence on the island. But they were discouraged. The islanders wanted no outsiders---and neither did Martin Ziegler. He could count on the islanders themselves to keep out intruders.

Since the island had never been attractive to tourists---a factor in Martin Ziegler's selection of it for his own refuge---the single third-class hotel remained as it had always been, an inn for commercial travelers and visiting bureaucrats of the government. The resident spies went to the wharf every day when the little chuffer brought the mail and goods from the mainland and took away shipments of wine when there were any. The spies observed the visitors who would be on their way to Martin Ziegler's villa, and then returned to their bridge game. The more eminent visitors, often recognizable from press photographs, would be met by M. Ziegler's chauffeur and footman and whisked up to the villa. Only the less important were likely to stop at the hotel. They would sign the registry, present their passports or cartes d'identite, and repair to their rooms, while the resident spies examined the registry and made their reports to their governments. On the occasions when visitors, very important, arrived by seaplane, the spies' bridge game was interrupted by the noise of the airplane coming in for a landing in the bay, and the spies, thus warned, would hurry to the pier and wait in the customs office for the visitors to be cleared. There was actually very little for the spies to do, aside from reporting to their governments on the arrivals and departures of M.

The Man Who Could Not Lose

Ziegler's visitors. But they all knew without saying so---they were, after all, competing spies---that their governments kept them on the island for one other purpose: every major government in Europe was waiting for the day when Martin Ziegler would leave the island.

That would be information worth sending. Some day it might come to pass that Martin Ziegler would be summoned to one of the capitals, or would feel that what he had to say could only be communicated in person. The capital he was most likely to visit was Rome, but that was not the problem of the island spies. The various governments would require of them only the information that he had left; the governments would know what use to make of the information, what his departure would signify. His destination would not be known by the spies, but it was imperative that they know he was going and had gone. Consequently there was always one spy, chosen by rotation, keeping watch on the bay against the arrival and quick departure of a speedboat or seaplane. The time would probably be late at night, and it could be assumed that M. Ziegler and his staff would take every precaution to avoid discovery. He would certainly not leave the villa in his large black Renault town car, but more probably in a gardener's truck or one of the Baby Renaults that belonged at the villa. The timing of his departure from the villa and the arrival of the seaplane would be precise and close, since the seaplane would be in communication with M. Ziegler's wireless station. The public telegraph office was not open at night and there was no telephone cable to the mainland, two facts which would give M. Ziegler a head start even if he were so unfortunate as to be seen departing. But that could not be helped. It was one of the hazards of espionage. The spies agreed among themselves that the ideal hour for departure, from M. Ziegler's point of view, was 22, ten o'clock. It gave him the widest margin, since the telegraph-cable office closed at six p.m., the manager-operator usually retired at nine p.m. and would refuse to be disturbed until morning. The owners of the two fast motorboats also retired early and therefore a charter to the mainland and telephone facilities was out of the question. Therefore M. Ziegler could be in Rome around midnight, have said what he had to say to Mussolini, and might even be back on the island before dawn. This also reminded the spies of the possibility that M. Ziegler could, with careful planning and luck, go to Rome and return without their ever being the wiser. It was a serious problem, and whenever one of the spies would revoke during their bridge game the others would comment sarcastically that the guilty party was worrying about their mutual concern. It was not the best job in the world, but it was one of the easiest, and they exercised a common vigilance; for they all knew that if they slipped up on M. Ziegler's departure, they would all have to become travel agents again.

26

In 1902, when Dorothy McCann became engaged to Martin Ziegler, he had not yet met her parents. Her father was an expert woodworker and master carpenter, employed in a boatyard near New Rochelle, and in frequent contact with the wealthy yacht owners for miles around. Peter McCann would come home from work and speak of the meetings he had with the rich. But his association with them was not a very good substitute for the real thing that Dorothy meant to have. Martin Ziegler made her forget her big ideas, but his own big ideas took their place. He was ambitious, he was on his way, and he was not afraid to spend money on her. If he was not a Vanderbilt or an Astor, he was handsome, well dressed, and already worth as much money as her

The Man Who Could Not Lose

father had saved in his lifetime. Martin's money was made in the stock market, by gambling, and if Dorothy McCann was not a Vanderbilt or an Astor, she was pretty, stylish, and fun, and when he took her out to dinner people would turn to look at her. Also, when they were alone she would listen to his own grand plans and understand his ambition. He bought her an expensive diamond and they had the meeting with her parents.

"Where are your people from, Mr. Ziegler?" said Peter McCann.

"I come from a little town in Minnesota," said Martin. "I was raised by an aunt. She made me finish high school and then I got a job in Chicago, office boy."

"Your parents are dead?"

"Both parents. My mother died when I was born, and my father put me to live with his sister. My father used to send my aunt money for my support, but I only saw him once or twice a year."

"What did he do for a living?"

"Well, I guess he took any job that came along. He was always on the go. I never heard from him much, but once a year he'd show up at my aunt's house. Not always at the same time, like Christmas. When he'd saved up some money, I guess. He used to come to see me, but after I began to grow up we never had much to talk about. We were strangers to each other. Then when I was fourteen he got married again, to a girl in Butte, Montana, and after that he didn't come to see me. He kept on sending my aunt money, but he had two children with the new wife and I guess she didn't want me. Anyway he was killed in a mining accident my last year in high. My aunt collected some money I guess from his insurance. Five hundred dollars, I guess it was. And she gave me a hundred of it to get me started in Chicago. Since then I've been pretty much on my own."

"Do you ever hear from your aunt?"

"All the time. Asking for money. She wants me to support her. But to tell you the truth, I supported her for eighteen years. Or my father did. He sent her enough for me and her, and she took all the money I used to earn from the time I was about seven or eight years old. She didn't lose anything on me. I don't owe her anything. By the time I was eighteen I should have had at least a thousand dollars that I'd earned, milking cows, delivering newspapers and jobs like that.''

"Then you don't think she's your responsibility?"

"You wouldn't either."

"I just wanted to know what obligations you had if you were married to Dorothy."

"Dorothy, and nobody else."

"Well, I guess there's a lot you're not telling me about your aunt."

"There is, but I don't see that it has anything to do with me marrying Dorothy. All you have to worry about is can I support Dorothy, and I can."

"So can I, and always have. That isn't what I worry about. It's what kind of man she wants to marry."

"I told you just about all there is to know. I can show you my bankbook, and I can get a statement from my broker that will show you a lot more than the bankbook will. Right now if I wanted to I could probably buy one of those boats you build, but I have other uses for my money. The yachts will come later."

"You have plenty of self-confidence, I'll say that for you."

"Listen, I could take what I have now and go back to Minnesota and be the richest man in town, or darn near. But the town I want to be the richest in is New York, and I'm a long way from that. But that's the direction I'm headed."

"I hope you succeed."

"Do you give your consent?"

"I'll let you know after I've thought about it."

"When will that be?"

"You mean when can you announce the engagement?"

The Man Who Could Not Lose

"No. We were thinking of getting married Saturday."

"Saturday? That's out of the question."

"Saturday's when we're getting married, Mr. McCann. If it isn't here, it'll be some place else."

"It'll be no place if you talk that way."

"Dorothy is twenty-one, and I got two weeks off from my job. I have two tickets for Niagara Falls right here in my pocket, the sleeper leaving Saturday night."

"Dorothy wouldn't skip off like that."

"Ask her."

"I won't ask her anything. I'll tell her that I don't approve of this marriage and won't give my consent."

"Well, then I don't see why we have to wait till Saturday. I thought I was doing you a favor, letting you be there when the knot was tied. But if that's the way you feel about it, we're both wasting our breath."

"Get out of my house!"

"All right. If it wasn't for Dorothy I wouldn't have been here in the first place," said Martin. He opened the door, and Dorothy was in the hall. "Your father's against me, so let's be on our way."

She looked sadly at her father, then quickly put her hand in Martin's arm, and they left the little house.

"I guess you heard it all," said Martin.

"Not all of it, some of it. Most of it, I guess. Did you say anything about your brother?"

"I never mentioned him."

"I thought maybe that might have been what made him cross."

"No, I never said anything about him."

"I was thinking maybe you should have."

"Why?"

"Well, then my father would have felt more kindly to you. If he'd known how you made something of yourself, even with your father

TWO BY O'HARA

neglecting you, and your aunt so mean, and your older brother no good at all."

"Wilbur wasn't a bad fellow. He was no worse than a lot of others, but he got caught with his hand in the till. And once you go to jail in a town like Seven Lakes, Minnesota, they never forget it. They never let you forget it, either. Wilbur wasn't a bad fellow."

"He was by comparison with you, though. You'd never do what he did."

"How do I know I wouldn't? Oh, I wouldn't for a measly two hundred dollars."

"You wouldn't for all the money in the world."

"All the money in the world? There is no such thing as all the money in the world, Dorothy. Nobody ever had that. But there's such a thing as a lot of money, like say $2,000,000. One for you and one for me. I'd hate to have that much put in front of me, to test my honesty."

"Just think of having a million dollars!"

"I never think about much else, except you."

"I wish Poppa wasn't cross."

"Now which do you want, sweetheart? A million dollars, or peace with your old man?"

"I'd like to have both."

"Well, maybe by the time I can give you a million your old man will come around. But he better do it before you get your million."

"Such big talk, Martin."

"I mean it. He better be polite to us before we're rich, or I won't be polite to him when we are."

Peter McCann did not come around, not when Martin Ziegler began to get rich, and not even when Dorothy had her first child. The men for whom Peter was building yachts were beginning to be aware of Martin Ziegler, more and more so as the years passed. He did not reveal his connection with Martin Ziegler, but Peter McCann had no trouble learning their opinion of his son-in-law.

The Man Who Could Not Lose

They expressed themselves guardedly, but apparently Martin Ziegler was admired and envied for his machinations in the stock market, while yet regarded as an outsider by the titans of the time. It was some comfort to Peter McCann to hear them predict disaster for his son-in-law, but he did not live to see the prediction come true, and after his death his widow was willing to accept an allowance from the man her husband despised. "The poor woman didn't have anything to do with it," said Martin. "I only saw her that one time and I don't hold it against her." The allowance also put an end to Mrs. McCann's remarks to the effect that worry over Dorothy had put Peter McCann in an early grave. Such remarks, made to Dorothy, only contributed to Dorothy's discontent when Martin neglected her for business.

The Zieglers had a charming house on West End Avenue, an English butler, a chauffeur, and a lovely little girl. Dorothy rode horseback in Central Park and went shopping in her town car and attended matinees, but she seemed not to know what to do with herself. Martin would come home in the evening and she would hear the names of the men he had seen during his day, sometimes at lunch, but Dorothy did not meet the men or their wives, although Martin was meeting some of the wives at the homes of business acquaintances. And when one of the wives---who, like Dorothy, did not know what to do with herself---began to prefer Martin to her husband and wanted to make a permanent arrangement, Dorothy for the first time realized that Martin had not always been the good husband she had thought him to be, and for which she had excused his preoccupation with business. The woman came to see Dorothy and was quite astonished at Dorothy's naivete. Later Martin denied everything convincingly. At least he was convinced that Dorothy accepted his version: the woman was a fool, had exaggerated common politeness, and was looking for revenge against her husband, who was notoriously unfaithful to her. Martin's kindness to her had been misinterpreted, but it taught him a lesson, he said. Never mix business and social life. This was somewhat dismaying to Dorothy, who had been hoping that Martin's business life would lead to a social life, but she could not argue against this new principle of Martin's, and since she had neither a business nor a social life to speak of, and did not enjoy playing cards, she sought and found adventure in the arms of an actor who lived not far away on West End Avenue. Without quite falling in love with Norman Seaforth, she had an affair with him that lasted until Martin Ziegler's 1922 crisis. "As if I didn't have enough trouble," said Martin. "You, and a matinee idol. And I never knew it all these years." Dorothy's success in keeping the affair secret seemed to irritate Martin as much as the affair itself. "I even backed one of his plays." This information was not startlingly new to Dorothy, who had learned it previously from Norman Seaforth.

"You'll never guess who's putting up the money for my new play," Norman had said. "None other than Martin K. Ziegler, who is interested in the leading lady's career. Your husband is a patron of the arts, no less. But so are you, darling. Thank you for the dressing gown."

It would not have been difficult in the circumstances for Dorothy to have stayed behind when Martin fled to Europe in 1922, but she knew it would be the last she would see of Josephine, and the child was the only interest in her life that transcended boredom and disillusionment and selfishness. Accordingly Dorothy made a credible gesture of standing by Martin in his trouble, and on his part the crisis had momentarily frightened him and he needed Dorothy for the first time in years. It was not a case of forgiving her for the affair with the actor, but rather of having the right to ask her to stand by him during the crisis, since she had been as guilty as he had ever been. In that respect Martin was following consistently his creed: to make a profit where a loss had seemed unavoidable; quid pro quo.

The Man Who Could Not Lose

27

In 1934 a new agent appeared at the island hotel, and he was a different sort of man from the others. For one thing, he did not join in the bridge game, and in spite of the fact that the agents who preceded him at the hotel had worked out mutually satisfactory procedures, he refused to participate in them. He even refused to admit that he was an agent, although the others pegged him as one within twenty-four hours of his arrival at the hotel. He carried a League of Nations passport, which may or may not have been genuine, and which identified him as Peter Zern, author and journalist. He had a square face, high cheek bones, small eyes, shiny skin, thin lips, heavy legs. He preferred to eat alone and he discouraged social overtures. He plainly did not trust the other agents, which was not remarkable, since they did not trust each other. But by his refusal to join in the mutual assistance pact he set himself apart from the others in a way that should have, but did not, prepare them for his subsequent outrageous conduct. This consisted of sneaking into the rooms of the other agents and examining their innocuous papers and possessions, and he also violated the tacit agreement between the agents and Martin Ziegler which made the villa and everything behind the walls sacrosanct. During their stay on the island not one of the agents had violated the agreement, but Peter Zern was caught one night outside the wireless station. Martin Ziegler's watchmen brought him to Martin.

"What did you think you would find?" said Martin.

The man did not reply.

"Oh, all right. But the next time you'll be shot for trespassing. That's why I'm not going to report you now. Next time we'll just shoot you. If I reported you, the gendarmes would know we were ready for you. I'd rather just shoot you. And of course you know that if I reported you to the police, Stalin would probably get rid of you for inefficiency. You're a stupid man."

Actually Martin Ziegler had no desire to shoot Peter Zern and create a fuss with the French police, since at that time the French and the Russians were viewing the Nazis with alarm, and a Soviet agent was considered to be spying for the right side. Peter Zern knew that, and within a week of his release Martin Ziegler learned that Zern was making inquiries into the death of Brooks, questioning the villa staff and the island natives. "Give him a good beating, put him out of circulation for a week or so," said Martin to his head watchman. The watchman was not told the reason for the beating, which was to remind Zern that Ziegler's staff was vigilant and Ziegler himself aware of Zern's snooping. Zern got no sympathy from his fellow agents, who easily guessed that he had not merely got into a quarrel with a fisherman, which was Zern's explanation for his bruises. They reported back to their governments that the Soviet agent was making their jobs more difficult and therefore worth higher pay, but the governments failed to respond.

28

The Brooks affair had blown over long before Zern's arrival on the island. The public had always accepted the accidental-fall-of-a-birdwatcher version of Brooks's death, and interested governments filed away their various reports. The British were well enough pleased that a reasonably credible explanation had been offered; it was not the kind of thing they wanted to make into a cause celebre. More than routine concern over the death of a national would only serve to remind financiers and all sorts of people that the Foreign

The Man Who Could Not Lose

Office and the War Office had Brookses all over the world---and it would also be an unnecessary reminder to the Brookses that even in the undramatic field of economic espionage there were hazards quite as perilous as those in the military. No man who was sending home confidential reports on Dutch rubber or Venezuelan tin would like to think that he might be pushed off a cliff in broad daylight. Also, it was next to impossible to plant an agent in the office of an important financier: a confidential secretary would have to be approached after he was well established, with an appeal to his patriotism, and while confidential secretaries may be susceptible to such appeals, they are not usually the kind of men who would welcome extreme danger. Therefore, the Brooks death caused no great sensation.

But it had its effect on the lives of Martin and Dorothy Ziegler. For nearly a year she was a prisoner at the villa. For part of that year she was Martin's mistress, a relationship that was a convenience for him, and so long as it remained so he did not bother to ask himself what it might be for her. He had no respect for the mind or integrity of any woman, just as he had occasional respect for the mind but never the integrity of any man. Martin Ziegler was a vigorous man who without realizing it had not had much luck in his women. One after another they had been easy for him (and he for them) and when the time came for him to change women, he changed them. It was not a difficult maneuver, since they all wanted the same thing from him, and he wanted the same thing from them, although what they wanted was not what he wanted. In his case it was sex and domination, in their case it was money in one form or another. He chose to believe that he had been in love with Dorothy McCann at the beginning, but it had not been love in any idealistic or selfless meaning of the word. Even his love for Josephine and Josephine's child, sexless though it was, needed the non-physical satisfaction of obedience and admiration, which took the place of overt sex. And in other respects his love for them resembled his love

TWO BY O'HARA

for Dorothy and the women who came after her, which in any analysis was not love at all.

This characteristic of Martin Ziegler's---incapability of love---made it possible for him to live on his island in comfort. As he had once told Francis Blackwell, he had everything there he needed. The physical need for women was satisfied by the Mrs. Raleighs and Dorothy. The need for companionship with other men did not exist in Martin Ziegler, although he considered himself a man's man. His visitors from the financial capitals stimulated him and satisfied him. But neither on his part nor theirs did anything resembling affection or friendship come into being. He had begun mature life with a native cleverness, shrewdness, about money matters, which developed as time went on into a kind of financial scholarship. He studied exchange until he was one of the world's leading experts, and in the course of his associations with the experts of other nations he improved his vocabulary, his manners, his taste in clothes, his knowledge of the social protocol in high places. He had certain natural assets: a good physique, the power of concentration, determination, ruthlessness, the long view, and a personal philosophy that caused him to examine his losses and defeats for salvage. If a thing had ever been good enough to invest in, there was always the chance that some good remained even when it seemed to be a total loss. Other men gave up too easily, and usually neither learned anything or salvaged anything---and remained, in Martin Ziegler's view---second-rate financiers. In 1922 he had not given up; he had run away, but he had run away with money enough to continue and expand. He considered his 1922 behavior a turning point in his career: if he had stayed in New York and, as Blackwell put it, taken his medicine like a man, he would have lived in humility for the rest of his life, taking jobs that were offered him out of kindness, but never again able or eligible to the position he sought in the financial community. But in Europe, operating from his island, he had made himself powerful and rich.

The Man Who Could Not Lose

For him the island was ideal; he saw things plain, uninfluenced and unprejudiced and unconfused and on his own. In the art or profession of arbitrage there was daily excitement, win or lose. He was well aware of his power and influence, that prime ministers and chancellors of exchequers asked themselves: "What does Ziegler think?" And men would be sent to the island to try to find out what Ziegler thought. And it was always *Ziegler*, not *Martin Ziegler*.

The great powers had told him often that they would be happy to have him come to their capitals; things could always be arranged with a maximum of secrecy, if that was what he wished, and assuredly with no embarrassment as to passports and such details. It was hardly likely that the United States of America would make trouble for a nation that admitted a fugitive of such standing. The official American view was that Martin Ziegler had made restitution in money and that there was the technical matter of legal disposal of the case, involving commission of a crime or crimes, and payment of income tax. But there were other expatriates in France who were in almost the same situation as Martin Ziegler and who were granted asylum by the French. Actually Martin Ziegler had declined numerous offers of citizenship in European countries, but he did not wish to involve himself with such finality, to restrict his operations in exchange for a passport he would probably never have to use. And at his age loyalty to a country was as unlikely to develop as loyalty to a woman. He had suffered no great pangs when he deserted the one, and he had never allowed fidelity to the other to interfere with his impulses.

In 1934 he had a large house party which was attended by high officials of the German and Italian governments, none of whom brought their wives. But women were present; the mistresses of some of the men. One of the women was a Viennese named Gerta Stiegel, the mistress of one of the newly powerful Nazis. She was young, in her early twenties, had been a minor actress and was sufficiently alert to political situations to take up with her Nazi friend. But Martin Ziegler in the present was worth any three Nazis of the future, and when the house party came to an end, Gerta remained on the island.

"How much longer is she staying?" said Dorothy, when the others had departed.

"Why?"

"Because if she stays, I leave."

"Well, that might solve a lot of things," said Martin.

"Oh, so that's the way it is?"

"So it seems, Dorothy. So it seems. You've been wanting to go, and all your friends will be glad to see you again."

"I have no friends."

"You will have. They're all very practical people, and I'm not going to be stingy with you."

"All right. But have I your permission to visit Josephine?"

"Yes. This time you have. I know she liked it when she heard you were living here again."

"I would like to be able to tell people that I'm coming back here."

"You want to be able to tell people you're Ziegler's wife. All right. But if I were you, I'd pick my new friends from among the Germans and the Italians. You'll be welcome in some places in England, but fewer and fewer as time goes by. I invited several Englishmen to this last party, but they were a little afraid to come. Oh, I could have filled the house with Englishmen, but not the ones I wanted. But all the Italians and Germans I invited were here."

"I noticed that."

"Yes, of course."

"One even left a souvenir of his visit. Fraulein Stiegel."

"That isn't exactly the way it was, Dorothy. One or two of the

The Man Who Could Not Lose

Italian ladies wanted to stay, too. But I preferred the fraulein. You know from experience how charming a Viennese can be. They're a lot like the French, but they're not fidgety. And they're like the English, but---well, of course Gerta is younger than the Englishwomen I've known."

"What was the name of that town in Minnesota?"

He grinned. "You can't make me mad, Dorothy. Minnesota was where I came from, and this was where I was always headed. Just like you and New Rochelle and that boatyard where your father made his $75 a week. If old Peter McCann could know how much you spend on perfume alone. . . . As much as he earned in a week, I guess."

"He'd still hold his nose, I'll bet."

"Yes, but you don't, and I don't. It's too late for us to pretend we're anything but what we are."

"What are we?"

"What we always wanted to be. And if the perfume smells bad to you, now that you have it, just remember that, that this is what you wanted. What if you'd married that actor, Norman Seaforth?"

"I never intended to marry him."

"But suppose you had? What would you be doing now? Sitting home while he was out philandering, and you'd make life hell for him by telling him what a great man I turned out to be. Well, here you are, Dorothy. Ziegler's wife."

"Those Nazis must have made you feel pretty good."

"They did. Hitler wants me to drop Mussolini and come in with him."

"Are you going to?"

"What a question, Dorothy! Would I give you the answer to that, just before you go visit your Italian daughter and her Italian husband?"

"Yes you might. You might want me to tell them that you were staying with Mussolini."

TWO BY O'HARA

"Oh, no. I want you to tell them that Hitler wants me, which is exactly what you *will* tell them. You'll let that slip somehow."

"Probably. Is that what you want me to do?"

"It doesn't make a great deal of difference. While the Nazis and Italians were here the Nazis never made any secret of how they felt about the Italians. I was surprised that the Italians would take such treatment."

"Who do you like best? Hitler, or Mussolini?"

"Ziegler is my man."

"And where is Ziegler going?"

"That's one thing I don't know."

"Where does Ziegler want to go?"

"Where does Ziegler want to go? Oh, that's such a big, big question, Dorothy. If they only didn't have to settle things with wars. If there was no such thing as war---if it was all fought with money against money, instead of guns against men and men against guns---then I could tell you where I want to go. But governments are men, and men go to war. They shoot each other. They're like women. In fact I always think of a government as a female. Nervous. Impulsive. Unreasonable. The sensible way is to have men like Ziegler in a competition with other men like Ziegler, and no one would be killed. We simply outguess each other, and the winner's country takes over the loser's country. Money over money." He paused. "If that was the way things were, I could be Mussolini and Hitler and Stalin and a lot of others will be fighting a war of blood, and while that's going on the men like Ziegler can't do much.* One of these days in the far future, it won't be necessary to kill each other. The wars will be peaceful wars, fought by Zieglers against Zieglers. I wish I could live long enough to get into such a war."

She listened with fascination if not comprehension. "Men will

*Thus in John O'Hara's typescript.

always be at each other's throats," she said.

"Not always. At least there'll be longer periods between wars. There will be a war in Europe within ten years, and then there will be a time of so-called peace when the Zieglers will be in power again. But wars will get worse, and people will refuse to fight them, and some day the Zieglers will produce a super-Ziegler and there won't be any need for war. The world will be one nation." He paused reflectively. "I'll say this for Hitler. He himself, or the people behind him, have begun to think about economic warfare on a bigger scale than it ever has been considered before. But there are too many countries now, too many nationalities, and as long as that's the case, there'll be those damn wars. Little by little there will be fewer countries, as the Zieglers put them out of existence in peacetime. Oh, I wish I had a son and he had a son. I'd show them how it could be done."

29

Peter Zern, although he would not join the bridge game, and was now not welcome in it, kept an eye on the players, and he was keeping an eye on them shortly after the preceding conversation when one of them was called to the telephone in the tiny lobby of the hotel. The agent spoke on the telephone, then returned to the bridge table but did not resume the game. He said something to the other players and they all rose, pausing only to study the cards in dummy and then each player put what remained of his hand in his pocket. All four then went out and proceeded to Ziegler's private pier. Presently an Isotta-Fraschini drove up and out stepped Dorothy Ziegler and personal maid. The maid and Dorothy,

TWO BY O'HARA

followed by chauffeur and footman with luggage, proceeded to Martin Ziegler's two-step commuting boat. Peter Zern, who had followed the bridge players, saw what was going on and hurried to a nearby pier and engaged a motor boat. Zern's boat was already slowly moving out of the harbor when the Ziegler boat roared seaward. The Ziegler boat soon overtook and passed the Zern boat, but Zern followed the fast boat all the way to the mainland, arriving there shortly after the Ziegler boat. But Dorothy and her maid and luggage took long enough to disembark for Zern to be able to observe her next move, which was to get in a Daimler limousine that was waiting on the mainland pier. Zern ran to the limousine.

"Please, Mrs. Ziegler?" he said.

"What is it?"

"Do you know me?"

"Yes. You're one of the men at the hotel."

"Thank you. I am in trouble. Will you help me?"

"I don't see why I should, and anyway I don't know how I can."

"Take me with you in the motor car."

"I wouldn't think of it," said Dorothy.

"Please, it is my life. I must get to Paris tonight."

"Then I couldn't help you anyway. I'm going to Rome." She got in the car, and Zern stood crestfallen as she rode away in the Daimler. But when she had turned the corner he grinned. He had found out where she was going. In the best of spirits and in leisurely fashion he entered a telephone booth. He returned to the island hotel and his chair in the lobby, and looked over at the bridge players with amused contempt.

30

Later in the evening of that day the Daimler arrived at the town house of Josephine Paladino. Dorothy and the maid got out of the car and entered the house. A man leaning against the wall a few yards from the entrance observed the arrival and the entrance to the house.

31

There was a party at the Paladino house. A youngish man was being especially attentive to Dorothy Ziegler. In the succeeding days he continued to be attentive to her at other parties and at his own flat. "Carlo, what do you do besides---this?" said Dorothy.

"This?"

"Yes, this. You're not the usual kind of gigolo. You seem to have money, and you're invited everywhere."

"The money, that might have come from my last lady. And the invitations---well, look at me. I'm presentable, I play very good tennis, and I have a small title. I add more to a party than a rich old man, especially for the ladies. I'm nothing very much, Dorothy. An adventurer, they sometimes call me."

He shook his head. "No, Dorothy. I am told they are all so suspicious of people like me. Here they all know. I should very much like to marry a woman of wealth, great wealth. No secret. And some day I shall. But in America they are so suspicious. In Europe there are many more widows of wealth, not little girls, but women. Some day I shall please one of them so much that she will propose marriage and I shall accept. And her sons and daughters

TWO BY O'HARA

will be pleased because Mama has a husband again. We will all understand each other, the sons and daughters and I. Financially speaking. They will not be afraid of me, because we will all understand beforehand what is to be my share. One-third. So much better for them than to have Mama spending it on young men she does not marry. And I shall be very careful as Mama's husband, because my one-third---you see?"

"Of course. But what do you live on meanwhile?"

"I don't need much to live this way. If a lady gives me a beautiful watch, I settle up with my tailor and then have credit again for two or three years. If another lady gives me a Maserati, I have pocket money for another three years. What else do I need money for? Rent? Nothing. Servants? One servant, underpaid. Food and wine? Other people wine and dine me all year long. You will surely give me a beautiful watch, or maybe a Maserati. Maybe you would even propose to me, Dorothy. And I would accept. Ziegler's wife! Now that would be perfect."

"I have no money of my own."

"But I hear you have."

"Well, I have, but not as much as I would have as Ziegler's widow."

Carlo smiled. "Is that what you were thinking when you shot him?"

"How did you know I shot him?"

"How I knew is not important, but when I heard it I always wanted to meet you. A rich American who would shoot her husband, and said to be quite beautiful. I went to Switzerland, hoping you would turn up there, but my trip was wasted. Ziegler fell in love with you again, yes? But now Ziegler has the little Nazi, Gerta." Carlo shook his head slowly. "I used to know Gerta."

"A girl friend of yours?"

"But of course. When she was nineteen or twenty. But she had nothing for me, and I had nothing for her. Nothing of permanent

The Man Who Could Not Lose

value, that is. The Nazis have put her there."

"I suspected that."

"Does Ziegler suspect that?"

"I don't know. He suspects everybody, and he may suspect her. He should, after all. But when he's tired of her he'll send her away."

"Don't be too sure of that, dear Dorothy. Ziegler is what? Fifty-six?"

"Fifty-seven."

"Gerta can be almost indispensable to men of fifty-seven. For young men there are always plenty of Gertas. For older men---well, Gerta is more popular with generals than with leftenants. In Paris there is a general who is ready to forgive Gerta if she will only come back to him. An important general, who should be happy to be rid of the little Nazi."

"Don't you like Nazis?"

"I love Nazis. I love the Fascisti. I love Mr. Roosevelt and Mr. Stalin. I want no big enemies, Dorothy. Only small ones."

"If you married me you might have a big enemy."

"Ziegler? I would not marry you if Ziegler said no. He is too big."

"You think Ziegler might want me to marry you?"

"That depends on Gerta."

"I didn't think she was that attractive. But of course I'm not a man."

"Happily not, for both of us."

"Thank you. So you're afraid of Ziegler?"

"Oh, yes. Very much. I have only one life. I do not wish to end it all alone in a small boat in Mare Nostrum."

She was struck by fear. "Don't say things like that."

"Why not? Because you are fond of me, and it is bad to say such things, Dorothy?"

"You're an Italian. You should know."

"I am half Italian."

"What is the other half?"

"My mother was a ballet dancer, with Diaghilev in the Ballet Russe."

"You're half Russian? Do they like that here?"

He smiled. "Yes. It explains my bad habits."

"Is she alive?"

"Oh, no. She committed suicide. She did not like the climate." He spoke with sardonic humor. "Russians come here to escape the cold, but my mother found Rome very chilly. Very, very chilly. If you stay here too long you may find it chilly, too."

"Why do you say that?"

"I shouldn't have said it. Forget it."

32

"Where did you learn to shoot?" said Martin Ziegler. "From one of your Nazi generals, or when you were a vaudeville artiste?"

Gerta called, "Pull!" and fired at a bluerock, smashing it on the rise.

"I was never a vaudeville artiste, as you call it."

"All right, a variety artiste."

"Never," said Gerta. "You have been misinformed."

"Listen, I don't mind what you were. I came up from nowhere myself."

"It is much easier to get reliable information about a famous person like yourself than an obscure one like me. I know all about you, Martin, but what you know about me---nothing." She smiled amiably. "And why do you care? I amuse you, isn't that enough?"

"More than enough. And I want you to believe me, I didn't have you looked up. But I know you were born in Prague, your father

The Man Who Could Not Lose

was a cellist in the opera house, your mother sold programs and once in a while played in crowd scenes. You took violin lessons till you were fourteen. Want the name of the man that gave you lessons? You ought to remember *him*."

She was disturbed, but trying not to show it. "You say you didn't have me looked up?"

"His wife left him on account of you, and he lost his job in the opera house because he struck the conductor. Jealousy. Then there was a baritone that you married. Divorced him. Let me see. In 1926 you lived in Paris and in French Morocco. A colonel in the French army. He had to give you up because a general became interested."

"What of it? Didn't you ask me to leave someone?"

"What I like is that you always improve yourself. You dropped the violinist for the conductor, the baritone for the colonel, the colonel for the general, the general for the Nazi, and the Nazi for me. What next, Gerta?"

"Pull!" she called, and this time she missed. She put down her gun. "Give me a cigarette."

"I don't smoke cigarettes, you ought to know that."

She fished in her shooting jacket and brought out a leather cigarette case, took one, and held it for him to light. "What was the purpose of reciting my dossier?"

"Someone is interested in telling me all about you."

"Your wife, I suppose."

"No. Not my wife."

"Who, then?"

"The information came anonymously."

"You pay attention to anonymous letters?"

"You bet I do. An anonymous letter in a case like this is bound to be accurate. If I found one mistake in it, I wouldn't trust the rest of the information, and the person that sent me this information wanted me to believe the whole thing, so he was sure of his facts."

"Clever of the great Ziegler."

"Moderately so. I have a hunch there will be more letters with more information."

"Well, I don't deny that there is more to be said. But what is the purpose? You said *he* was sure of *his* facts. I will tell you something, Ziegler. Not one of the men that he mentioned knew so much about me as he told you. What he told you is true, and more complete than my gentlemen friends ever knew. But your informant may be telling you true things now in order to tell you one big lie that you cannot verify."

"I thought of that, naturally. But I know what it's going to be, don't you?"

"What is it going to be?"

"In the next letter I will be informed that you are a Nazi agent."

"Quite possibly. And what will you do then?"

"What I am doing now. Nothing. Of course you're a Nazi agent. But if I got rid of everybody that was an agent around here, I'd have no one to talk to. And in your case, of course, the conversation is very pleasant indeed."

"I hope you continue to find it so."

"Is that all you have to say?"

"What else is there to say? You are convinced that I am working for the Nazis. I could not change your mind. But what am I doing for them? I admit that I have been paid for little bits of information in the past. But I have no understanding of what makes you so important. And what else is there for me to report to the Nazis? That you have visitors? That you go for a swim twice a day? That you have a high wall about your place? They surely know all that."

"Long since."

"Then what is there for me to find out?"

"What you've already found out. That I'm more fond of you than I've ever been of any other woman."

"And yet I'm sure I would have no influence over you in whatever it is you do."

The Man Who Could Not Lose

"None whatsoever. But the Nazis may be hoping you will have."

"*I* am hoping that, Martin."

"Why?"

"Because I should like to stay here forever."

"Are you in love with me, Gerta?"

"Oh---what do we mean when we talk about love, people like you and me?"

"We *could* mean *love*."

She shook her head. "You don't believe that, and neither do I. Too bad, too. But what is there for a woman like me? You have seen my record, and not all of it. I live grand luxe, but I have no money. No man would want to marry me or thinks of it. In a few years my face and my body will not be pretty any more, and even now, Martin, the competition is fierce. Oh, it is fierce." She smiled. "These younger ones are so attractive, the horrible creatures. And the older ones, those that have survived are much more clever than I."

"I've seen the older ones and the younger ones. I still like you best."

"For how long? A year? Two years?"

"Who knows? How long would you stay interested if I lost everything? And there are plenty of people who would like to see that I do."

"You would not lose everything. This thing that you know how to do, that you are famous for. You could lose everything and be rich again in a year. You have a power. I have heard them speak of you. Ziegler says. Ziegler is going to. I hear that Ziegler." She laughed. "I used to think of a hunchbacked old man, with a skullcap on his head, bent over a desk, surrounded by books and papers and men with machine guns." She laughed again. "Ah, Ziegler, you were a great disappointment to me. You are a *man*!"

He grinned.

"I think I love you. I want to. That's it. I never wanted to love anyone before." She turned sober. "This is the different thing, Ziegler. I never wanted to love anyone before."

"Is that what it is? It may be." He put his arm about her shoulders and they walked slowly to the house.

33

The black-shirted officers with their ivory-handled daggers and Baretta pistols spoke sharply to the Paladino butler. "Mrs. Ziegler, bring her to us."

"Yes, gentlemen?" said Dorothy, when she joined them.

"Sit down, Signora. Over there. You have been seeing a great deal of one Carlo Robelli. It will be useless to deny that fact."

"I don't deny it, even if you gave me a chance to."

"How much money have you given him?"

She laughed. "How much money have I given him? Do you realize that my husband is Martin K. Ziegler, a close friend of your Duce?"

"If we did not realize that these questions would not be asked here. They would be asked elsewhere, where you would not be so comfortable. Please answer the question."

"I'll do nothing of the kind. Now leave here, pronto. And I shall telephone the chancellery as soon as you leave."

"Our visit here is known already to Il Duce. First question, how much money did you give Robelli?"

"None of your business."

"Refuses to answer first question. Second question, when did you last see Robelli?"

"My answer is the same."

"Refuses to answer second question."

"And any others you ask me."

"Third question, names of men and women you saw at Robelli's apartment."

"No answer."

"No answer to third question. Fourth question---"

"No answer."

"Fourth question, have you ever stolen any papers from General Paladino, your son-in-law?"

"No! How dare you!"

"Denies stealing papers from General Paladino. Fifth question, are you a member of the Communist Party?"

"I refuse to answer."

"Refuses to answer Number 5. Number 6, how much money have you contributed to enemies of the Fascist government?"

"Oh, stop this silliness."

"Disrespectful reply to Number 6. Question Number 7, who is Marie Pitot?"

"You know perfectly well who she is, she's my personal maid."

"Identifies Pitot woman. Number 8, how long has Pitot been a member of the Communist Party?"

"Ask her."

"Evasive answer, indicating knowledge of Pitot's membership in anti-Fascist underground."

"That's not true, and you know it."

"Nine, what was the nature of the message you brought from the Soviet agent on the Island of Cedars?"

"You're out of your minds."

"Insulting evasive answer. Ten, how long has Peter Zern been your lover?"

"Now you're being funny. I never heard of Peter Zern, and I don't think you did either."

"Denies knowing Soviet Agent Zern!" The interrogator smiled

superciliously at his companion. "Denies knowing the fellow. Mrs. Ziegler, you were seen in earnest conversation with Zern in a Daimler motor car a few hours before you came to Rome. Five witnesses in addition to the maid Pitot and the chauffeur Muraschi."

"Oh, is that who he was?"

"Admits having conversation with Soviet agent. But you still deny he was your lover?"

"Yes, I deny it."

"Why do you deny it? You have had lovers and made no secret of it. Why do you deny that Zern was your lover? Is he one that Mr. Ziegler would object to?"

"Oh, I think he would. He doesn't like Communists."

"But you do?"

"I don't know any."

"You know Zern, a dangerous Communist agent."

"If you say so."

"Then why don't *you* say so? It would make things easier for us and for you."

"I don't want to make things easier for you."

"That is obvious. Next question."

"Question Number 11?"

"Question Number 11, yes, and I warn you to be careful of your answer. What do you know of a plot to assassinate Il Duce?"

"Nothing at all."

"Denies knowing of plot to assassinate Il Duce. Do you deny that you gave money to Robelli?"

"I don't deny it. I refuse to answer."

"Because in your mind you connect the two things, the plot to assassinate Il Duce and the money you gave Robelli."

"That isn't a question, it's a statement. There must be thousands of Italians that want to assassinate Mussolini."

The Man Who Could Not Lose

One of the officers leapt forward and slapped her face. "You have insulted the Fascist state."

"And committed high treason. You will come with us."

The officers took her by the wrists and pulled and pushed her to their car. The butler, from a hiding place, watched them go.

34

One of the blackshirt officers, now in civilian clothes, was admitted with another Italian to Martin's office study. On the way in they showed that they are acquainted with Martin's new secretary, an Englishman named Motley, but they pretended not to know him when they were in Martin Ziegler's presence.

The blackshirt, a man called Contino, did all the talking. "Good morning, sir, I am Commendatore Contino, this is my assistant, Mr. Brazzi."

"I have met Mr. Brazzi. I didn't know he was your assistant."

"Well, he is not really my assistant, but I outrank him in the Fascist chain of command."

"Yes, go ahead with whatever you have to say. I'm a busy man, Commendatore Contino, and in my business hours I don't like to be interrupted by the military. Nothing personal. It's simply that I don't often see eye-to-eye with soldiers. In my free time, of course, I enjoy their company, but I don't consider this my free time. However, it must be important, so, as I said, go ahead."

"I respectfully suggest that it might have been worth your while to have spent more time with the military, sir."

"And I respectfully suggest that I'm the best judge of how to spend my time. Also, that Premier Mussolini agrees with me."

"Not today, dear sir."

Martin Ziegler looked at his wristwatch. "Ten minutes, gentlemen, as a courtesy to my friend Il Duce," he said. "But only as a courtesy to *him*."

"Very well, sir. Do you know the whereabouts of Mrs. Ziegler at this moment?"

"I think she's in Rome. At our son-in-law and daughter's town house."

"I have the unpleasant task of informing you that she is in custody, in Rome. Please do not lift your telephone, it will be a waste of time. Il Duce will not receive your call."

Martin Ziegler took his hand off the instrument. "She's under arrest? What for?"

"She is not under arrest---yet. She is in custody to answer certain questions concerning a Communist plot against the Fascist state. The degree of a charge against her would be high treason."

"You've got the wrong woman."

"We disagree. When she left your boat she was seen in conversation with the Communist agent Zern. She employs as personal maid a notorious Communist, Pitot, who traveled with her to Rome and is now under arrest. Pitot has admitted her connection with the plot to assassinate Il Duce---"

"Assassinate him?"

"I have not finished. And your wife's lover, Robelli, has been receiving money from your wife that was contributed to the anti-Fascist movement."

"My wife is not a Communist, and the money she gave her lover wasn't enough to finance a revolution. I know how much money she has, and if she gave all of it to such a cause it still wouldn't be enough."

"You knew she gave this money to Robelli?"

"I assume that he's no different from any other gigolo, although

The Man Who Could Not Lose

I've never heard of him till this minute. But a million dollars wouldn't overthrow Mussolini, and that's all she has."

"No money will destroy the Fascist state, but a million dollars would more than pay for an assassination."

"But how do you know she gave him a million dollars? The money is not in cash, it's in securities in a Swiss bank, and that can be checked in five minutes."

"We have not claimed that she gave a million dollars to the assassination. But we know that she gave money to Robelli, money which Robelli then turned over to his fellow-conspirators."

"I suppose it would be foolish to ask where Robelli is now."

"He has gone on a long journey."

"I'll bet. Well, what do you want me to do now?"

"First to divorce your wife."

"Yes, but that's not all. That's too easy. Let me guess. You would like me to divorce her so that she wouldn't have my protection? Right? Then what happens to her?"

"She will no longer be your responsibility."

"Very delicate. I turn her loose, then you do whatever you please. Why the delicacy?"

"Because certain high authorities would like to maintain the same excellent relations with you, but without your wife."

"I'm not overly fond of my wife, but I don't like the idea of turning her over to the wolves. And I know my daughter wouldn't like it."

"Your daughter is the wife of General Paladino, and he will obey our orders."

"So then all I have to do is divorce Dorothy."

"You have every reason to in any event."

"I have. It's just a question of how much I want to. Will you let her leave Italy if I do?"

"We promise nothing."

"And even if you did, eh?"

TWO BY O'HARA

"She will be allowed to leave Italy if you, on the other hand, promise she will be given no more money."

"She can keep her million, but no more? The income from a million won't support her present mode of living."

"But she will not be your wife, and it is still a large amount of money in Europe."

"You know, I don't think Dorothy was mixed up in any Communist conspiracy, but your proposition does have some interesting features to it."

"Then you agree?"

"I would like to speak to Premier Mussolini."

Contino shook his head. "You may speak to Count Ciano, but Il Duce is much too disturbed."

"By which you mean he may say things he'll regret."

"Il Duce has always placed the highest value on your friendship. The wife of a lesser man would not have received such consideration."

"In other words, she'd probably be dead. Well, that's true. She ought to be grateful for that, although I don't suppose she will be. All right, I'll divorce her. How shall we handle it?"

"She will be deported immediately. The divorce will be arranged by the lawyers."

"No harm is going to come to her. I want to be sure of that."

"You may be sure of that."

"Does she know about Robelli and his long journey?"

"She will be told. That he has gone away. She will not be unhappy to leave Italy."

The Man Who Could Not Lose

35

"Mrs. Ziegler is on the telephone from Paris," said Motley.

"I don't want to speak to her," said Martin Ziegler.

36

"Your mother is a fool," said Paladino.

"I know, but I feel sorry for her," said Josephine.

"Then pray for her, but have nothing more to do with her, or I'll be sent to some outpost in Somaliland and you and the children with me."

37

The great couturier himself appeared before Dorothy Ziegler, waving his hand to dismiss the vendeuses who were hovering nearby in his salon. "Madame, we have been friends for so many years. But the coat is priced at $15,000, and Madame's account is unpaid these many months."

"It always was, Jules. My bills were always paid once or twice a year."

"In other times. But one hears things. A little on account? Say 50% of the outstanding bill?"

"My husband---"

"I have had a letter from Mr. Ziegler---unless, of course, Madame has a new husband, in which case. . . ."

"I have no new husband."

38

"I'll take it," said Dorothy, indicating the splendid new town car.

"Madame will write us a cheque?" said the salesman.

"For the down payment."

The man shook his head. "Oh, I'm afraid we had in mind the full payment."

39

The banker sniffed his boutonniere. "It is not a very good time to sell securities, Mrs. Ziegler. These were worth $500 a share six years ago, but $35 is our final offer today."

40

"Pearls?" said the merchant. "Oh, I know these pearls. I sold them to Mr. Ziegler many years ago, but today the clasp is more valuable than the pearls."

41

Paul Giraud smoothed back his hair. "You see, Dorothy, I am in no position to go against Martin's wishes. I don't own the steamship line. Martin has owned it, and me, for several years. If I displease him, I will be looking for a job tomorrow, and at my age. . . . You have a very comfortable fortune, I'm told. You must learn to live within your income."

42

"Yes, I *have* been avoiding you, Dorothy," said Von Lemnitzer. "And it was unfair of you to come here this way. My wife and my children and I myself would be in serious danger if the Nazis find out that I have seen you. I don't believe that you are a Communist, but the Nazis believe it."

43

"She refuses to believe that the money has stopped," said Paul Giraud. "She has been spending capital, and I mean spending it."

44

"Is this real?" said the young man, holding up her hand and examining the ring.

"Of course it's real," said Dorothy.

"It must be fifteen carats," he said.

"Twenty, I think," said Dorothy.

"Twenty carats! What I could do with that!"

"Take it."

"You mean it?"

"I always mean everything I say. Here, you cheap little man, take it and go."

"Not so cheap, twenty carats, hein?"

"I consider it cheap if it gets rid of you."

"You can't insult me, old woman," he said. He left with the diamond.

45

The Paris house was apparently unoccupied, but singly and in twos and threes men and women were being admitted at the front door. It was evening, and the woman got out of the taxi, paid the driver, and rang the bell.

"Who are you?" said the man who opened the door.

"Who are you?" said the woman.

"Let me see your card," said the man.

"Let her in," said a second man. "It's her house."

Dorothy Ziegler was admitted and made her half-drunken way

past groups of men and women who were waiting for the Party meeting to begin. "Hurray for Stalin," she cried, and laughed. The men and women stared at her coldly, and a large bearded man wearing a beret separated himself from a group and took her by the arm, up the stairs.

"Thank you, comrade," she said. She entered her room, and he took the key from the door and locked it on the outside.

46

The meeting ended, and the man in the beret went up to her room and unlocked the door. "There is a comrade from America who wishes to see you."

"How nice of the comrade from America, but I don't know any comrades in America. Have a drink?"

"I do not drink. Here is the comrade."

An American, sixty-ish, hatless, short bristly hair, blue flannel shirt, nondescript necktie, old suit, entered and closed the door behind him. He studied her for a moment. "So you're Dorothy," he said.

"Yes, I'm Dorothy. Who are you?"

"I wouldn't of known you from your pictures I saw in the papers."

"That doesn't sound very complimentary."

"It aint meant to be. Do you know who I am?"

"I asked you once."

"I'm your brother-in-law."

TWO BY O'HARA

She shook her head. "Somebody's brother-in-law, comrade. But not mine. I never had a---Wilbur! Are you Wilbur?"

"I'm Bill Ziegler. Yes."

"Sit down and have a drink. Do you drink champagne?"

"I drink anything if it's free. I just wanted to have a look at you. You're a real mess, you are."

"I know. One too many Zieglers, I guess. Well isn't this nice? Martin's brother a commie, and he doesn't even know you're alive. That's irony for you, isn't it, Wilbur?"

"Call me Bill, that's what I go by."

"What do you do for the Party, Bill?"

"That's for me to know and you to find out."

"Oh, you're a real hick, aren't you?"

"Insults from you brush right off."

"One thing I must say, Bill, if I had to marry a Ziegler, I got the pick of the litter. But why are you a commie? Why aren't you a Mussolini boy? Martin is, and I'm sure he'd be glad to put in a good word for his older brother."

"Their time will come, my brother and Mussolini."

"They think it's almost here. But not the same way you do, I guess. Oh, this is delicious. You being a commie, I mean. Not the champagne. The champagne is too warm. And you're too cold."

"I just wanted to see what one of you was like, and particklery one I was related to. Useless and decadent."

"You don't have to be unpleasant. It's my house, and I think it's very nice of me to let you have your meetings here."

"You don't have no choice in the matter, what I hear."

"Well, I suppose that's true. I asked them to have their meetings some place else. No servants will stay. But they refused. So I guess I have no choice. Oh, well, if you want the house it's all right with me. I'm tired of Paris anyway. But thank you for coming to see me, Wilbur. I must get word to Martin, even if I can't see his face when he hears about you."

47

Europe proceeded on its way to war, and every step of the way seemed to be a vindication of Martin Ziegler's judgment as the Axis powers called all the turns from Munich to Warsaw, and the rough moment he had during France's early resistance passed quickly and triumphantly for him with the creation of the Vichy government. Gerta remained as his mistress, the first he had kept for more than a year. Stories of the collapse of Dorothy Ziegler no longer held any interest for Martin Ziegler or anyone else; she was reported to be penniless after the German occupation and the quick seizure of her possessions, and she seemed to disappear in an alcoholic haze.

So went the lives of Martin and Dorothy and Gerta until 1945 and the inescapable signs of the Axis collapse. Then Martin turned up in Zurich, leaving Gerta behind to face the wrath of the liberated French.

"There are not many places for you to go, Martin," said his friend Schlosser, the Swiss banker.

"No, not many places left," said Martin. "At least not for the present."

"That being the case, you will behave yourself while you're here," said Schlosser.

"Oh, I intend to behave myself."

"We stayed out of the war, and we intend to stay out of the peace, if you know what I mean. In other words, Martin, our government is particularly anxious to be as neutral as ever, if not more so, and we wouldn't like to have a visitor use our hospitality in such a way as to interfere with our relations with *all* other nations."

"Put your mind at rest. I don't need any more money than I have here in Switzerland, and this is a wonderful place to look down at the world making a mess of itself."

"We know you have enough money. It isn't that that we might

TWO BY O'HARA

worry about. For a rich man you've never been very extravagant. But a man like you, with your special ability and considerable means at his disposal, could find ways to take advantage of the world situation."

"You're politely telling me not to over-extend myself. I won't. At least not for the present, and when I do you'll surely know about it."

"We surely will, and then you had better have your next country carefully selected, because you will be unwelcome in Switzerland."

"All these things are things you and I know without having to state them so plainly. I wonder why you are taking the trouble?"

"Because we have had to arrest your brother."

"My brother? My brother is dead."

"Where did he die, and when?"

"Well, I don't know, but I've always assumed he was dead. I've never heard from him, not in forty years."

"He has been here all through the war years, spying on the American spies."

"Why have you arrested him now?"

"For violations of Swiss neutrality."

"I imagine that can cover a multitude of sins."

"It can. We have also arrested a man named Zern. For the same reason. Zern, as you know, is a Russian agent and so was your brother. Naturally I don't speak for my government, but I have heard that you are possibly undergoing a change of heart in regard to the U.S.S.R. If that's the case, the Swiss government realizes that you would like to have men you can trust in Switzerland, and your brother and Zern would qualify."

"Zern used to spy on me, and I tell you I haven't seen my brother in forty years."

"Yes, you tell me that, but fortunately I am not compelled to believe you."

The Man Who Could Not Lose

"I see your point. I'd be just as suspicious as you are. What happens to my brother?"

"He will be deported to the U.S.A., and Zern will be sent to Poland."

"You must know that I haven't seen either of them."

"Unfortunately, all we know is that we don't know whether you've seen them or not. But we are leaving nothing to chance. So long as you behave, or so long as we are not aware that you have misbehaved, you may stay, unmolested."

"I'll be careful. I like it here."

48

"I have been given permission to see my brother," said Martin Ziegler.

"We have been expecting you, Mr. Ziegler," said the official. "I shall remain with you during the interview."

Wilbur Ziegler entered the room, and the brothers faced each other, trying to find things they remembered. "I guess you're Wilbur, but I wouldn't have known you."

"I'd have known you."

"From pictures, maybe."

"No, you haven't changed as much as I have. But you've had it easier all your life."

"I suppose I have. But I was always smarter than you, Wilbur. I never would have stolen $200."

"No, two million."

TWO BY O'HARA

"Exactly. So you're a commie."

"Didn't Dorothy tell you? Your wife?"

"She wrote me a letter to that effect, but it didn't make any more sense than anything else she wrote."

"What happened to her?"

"Search me, Wilbur. She just disappeared."

"She was decadent, like the rest of you, but maybe not hopeless."

"Do you want some money?"

"Yes."

"How much do you need?"

"How much have you got? I don't want $500, if that's what you were thinking of. But I'll take all you'll give me for the Party."

"If I decide to give money to the Party I don't do it through you."

"You can't buy your way into the Party."

"Yes I can. And I can buy my way in without giving up a cent. That's because I always was and always will be smarter than you, Wilbur. I've thought about your Party, and what I think isn't much. It's full of men like you. But Russia, the U.S.S.R., that's another matter. I always prided myself in making a profit out of a loss. I went along with Hitler and Mussolini and lost, but I might go along with Stalin and die ahead of the game. That's all I care about any more, Wilbur. You wouldn't understand that, but it's been my philosophy all my life. The United States doesn't want me, and I don't want the United States. But there's still Russia, and they can certainly use me now. They've captured all those German scientists and taken them to Russia, not because they like Germans, but because they need scientists. And they need people like me, too. There are only about four men like me left in the world, and they have one of them, a Chinese gentleman. The others are opposed to Russia. So this may turn out to be the best thing that ever happened to me. But you wouldn't understand any of that, Wilbur. You're a $200 man and you always were. The whole trouble with Russia so far has been too many $200 men. Well, I'll send you some cigars. You used to like cigars, and that's about all there is left for you, Wilbur."

49

"I wondered how long it would take you to get here," said Martin Ziegler to the Russian ambassador.

"Purely a courtesy call, Mr. Ziegler---"

"Stop that nonsense. You are here as a messenger boy because Stalin wants me to come to Moscow. Stalin wants my brains. All right. You make the arrangements and I'll go to Moscow."

"It is understood, of course, that---"

"Nothing is understood. If you mean that I'm going to give Stalin my money, the answer is no. I will go to Moscow and work for Stalin as financial adviser, and he will make me comfortable. If I make a mistake, he can shoot me, but he'll never get the money I've made. That's mine, and if Stalin does shoot me, then the Swiss government will be that much richer. If Stalin wants to send me back here, I'll at least have the money to play with. But as long as I'm happy in Moscow, I won't miss the money. In other words, my friend, I am not going to turn it over to Stalin and get lost in the shuffle after he has my money. I will go to Russia to work."

"That is precisely what I was instructed to say to you, sir. You will be treated with the same respect and generosity as the German scientists who realized that the Soviet Union is the true home of the---"

"Yes, yes, yes, yes."

TWO BY O'HARA

50

The last of the children had gone home for the day, and Libby Stanley sat at her desk and took a folded letter out of her skirt pocket. She held it in front of her, but it was a token gesture; she did not need to read the letter again.

"You ready to go, Lib?" said Mary, another teacher who was her friend. "Is something the matter?"

"No, I guess not. This is what they call finding out in time."

"John Blackwell?"

"John Blackwell," said Libby, handing Mary the letter. She read the letter:

Dear Libby:

I have not written you because I did not like what I had to say, but it is no use putting it off any further. I am not coming out to Chicago to see you, because that will only make it all worse. If I go to Chicago, I might not be able to tell you that there are so many things against our getting married that there hardly seems to be anything in favor of it. After we had been married a while, after the romantic phase was over, I would not be able to forget that Martin Ziegler was your grandfather and that I hate and despise him and everything he stood for. It is not only that he was responsible for my grandfather's death, but there are so many other things I object to, but you are also loyal to him in a strange way and our marriage would not last. There has never been a divorce in our family and I do not want to get married with the feeling that if I make a mistake, there is always that way out.

I should have said all this before, when I first began to realize that Martin Ziegler could still have such a hold over you, a man whom you had not seen in so many years.

Needless to say I wish you happiness and I am truly sorry that I will not be the one to share it with you, but that man would be like a cloud hanging over us and our happiness would be short-lived.

Sincerely,
John Blackwell

The Man Who Could Not Lose

"Yes," said Mary. "It *is* finding out in time."

"Oh, well, it is for him, too. And I'm sure he's right."

"It's no consolation now, but you'll find someone else, Libby."

"Of course I will. Tomorrow, maybe. Next week. But I'll always have to tell them who my grandfather was, and I'm not so sure I'd want to marry anyone that would think nothing of my being Martin Ziegler's granddaughter."

"You shouldn't marry anyone that doesn't want you for yourself alone, regardless of who your grandfather was, good or bad."

"I know, but John Blackwell is right. My grandfather does have a hold over me, and always will. Most people are luckier than I am. Their illustrious ancestors were good men. Mine was everything bad---except to me. I wonder what he's doing. I wonder if he's still alive."

THE END

Far From Heaven
A MELODRAMA

ABOVE
John O'Hara with his MG-TC

OPPOSITE
*John O'Hara "in an act of defiance
to the anti-cigarette-smoking bluenoses"*

OVERLEAF
John O'Hara's plan for FAR FROM HEAVEN

Act I – Scene 1 – Saloon; Fallon, Moore,
Mona, Tony, et al., and
John J. Sullivan

P.|28| Scene 2 – the same

P.|38| Scene 3 – the apartment; John
and Alice; day after
Scene 2;

P. |62| Scene 4 – Late that night; John
& Alice, after he has
stood her up

Act II – Scene 1 – Several weeks later.
|P.70| Afternoon. Making bets.
Spider's visit; Mr
Benjamin's visit;
Peggy's visit;

|P.101| Scene 2 – later, several nights
later; the Beating;
Alice Farewell

|P.115| Scene 3 – John tries to make a bet.
calls Peggy, has a fight
with Spider; Mona's
visit

Act III |P.136| – Scene 1 – Apartment, next day, after
John and Mona have reunited
Visit of Roy Fallon

|P.145| Scene 2 –

Act One
SCENE
1

The Scene is the backroom of a dingy saloon in the Chelsea district of New York City. The Time is the late Thirties. At Rise a group of men and two women, some standing, some sitting, are having drinks of beer and highballs. They are actually not one group but several, and there is nothing but confusion and noise until RAY FALLON, *a portly youngish middle-aged man, takes a place standing behind a table Up Center and raps on the table with a tin ash tray.*

RAY FALLON: All right, everybody, take your seats. Take your seats, please. Everybody sit down. This meeting is now called to order.

PEGGY MOORE* (*a blowzy middle-aged woman*): By who?

RAY: By me. Sit down Peggy.

PEGGY: Who elected you chairman, I'd like to know.

RAY: I did. I elected myself. Do you have any objections?

PEGGY: Sure I have objections---

MONA DEVLIN (*a handsome woman in her thirties who has seen*

---

*This character's name changes from *Betty* to *Peggy* on p. 26 of John O'Hara's typescript (p. 120 here), and remains *Peggy* thereafter. Her name is printed as *Peggy* in all instances here. But see p. 159 where O'Hara changed her full first name from *Margaret* to *Elizabeth*.

better days): She always has objections. Who remembers a time when Peggy didn't have objections?

TONY FLANAGAN: Me. I can remember she didn't put up any objections when---no, I take it back. She always put up some objections. Peggy's a very objectionable woman.

PEGGY: Ah, shaddap.

RAY: Does anybody besides Peggy have any objections to me being chairman?

CHORUS: No, no, no, no.

TONY: Carry on, old boy.
    But be careful who you carry on with. Yak yak yak yak yak.

SPIDER RATTIGAN: I got a question I want to ask. Will you shut up and listen to me for a minute?
    Here's my question. I got no objection to Ray being chairman of this meeting. But I want to know this: does that mean Ray gets to be the permanent chairman?

RAY: I'll answer that, Spider.
    The answer is no.
    I don't want to be permanent chairman. As soon as we finish up this meeting I'll step down. You can elect a permanent chairman, and I don't wish to be a candidate.

PEGGY: How did you get to be temporary chairman? Will somebody answer me that?

RAY: I'll answer it. I appointed myself chairman because it was me that called the meeting.

PEGGY: Are you paying for the drinks?

RAY: The hell I am. The house is.

PEGGY: Then why should you be chairman?

MONA: You didn't have to come to the meeting.

Far From Heaven

PEGGY: I was invited, just the same as anyone else.

SPIDER: Nobody'd be damn fool enough to offer to buy the drinks for this crowd.

PEGGY: Are you casting aspersions? I don't think you ever bought a drink in your life.

DICK SHERIDAN: Let's get the meeting started. I have to go uptown. I have to be at rehearsal at five o'clock.

PEGGY: Rehearsal for what?

DICK: A record date.

PEGGY: How about taking me with you? I just want to see if Tommy Dorsey'll remember me.

TONY: If he ever saw you he would.

PEGGY: If he ever saw me. He give me first prize in a Charleston contest.

DICK: I can't take you to rehearsal---

TONY: I can't take her. Period.

RAY: Are we going to get this thing started or aren't we? Dick isn't the only one has to go to work.

CHORUS: Yeah, let's get started. Let's cut the comedy. Let's start.

RAY: All right. If everybody'll keep quiet for five minutes, I'll state the purpose of why I called this meeting.

PEGGY: Everybody knows why you called the---

DICK: I don't.

FRANK GAFFNEY: Neither do I.

TONY: To see Peggy Moore do the Charleston.

RAY: Oh, come on, Tony.

TWO BY O'HARA

The purpose of this meeting---and for Christ's sake shut up---is as follows. As you all know, our popular leader, John J. Sullivan, leader of this district and one of the more popular leaders in the City---New York---

TONY (*chanting*): County New York, State of New York.

RAY (*continuing*): ---is once again a free man, having earned his release from prison last Thursday. In other words, John is no longer a guest of the State.

TONY: To put it nicely.
Were you talking to him since he got out?

RAY: No, I did not have that opportunity. Thursday morning he had his brother Joe meet him with a car, and then they drove off somewhere.

TONY: Where to?

RAY: I'm not privileged to have that exact information.

WILLIE DEVLIN: Why didn't he come home? When I got out I could hardly wait to come home, see my parents and friends, the old gang.

RAY: Joe told me John didn't want to come home right away. He wanted to go somewhere and get that prison smell out of his nostrils first.

FRANK: I'll bet a dollar there's one person here knows where he went.

(*They all turn to* MONA.)

MONA: Don't ask me.

WILLIE: I can vouch for Mona. She don't know where he went.

FRANK: Well, if Mona don't know, nobody does.

MONA (*not proud of her ignorance*): If he wanted me to know, he'd have told me. But you gotta respect a man's privacy.

PEGGY: A little burnt up because she don't know, if you ask me.

MONA: I don't happen to be the kind of a woman that goes chasing after a man if he doesn't want to tell me where he is. I come this far without being a man-chaser. Of course some women are different constituted. Like I heard of one---trying to think of her name--- she's so fond of the sea air.

PEGGY: Now you watch what you're saying.

MONA: She's so fond of the sea air she's always stowing away on the tugboats.

RAY: Order, order!

PEGGY (*simultaneously*): What's worse? Going for a ride on a tugboat, or lushing it up with some Frenchman off the Ro-*cham*-bo?

RAY: If you two don't shut up, I'll kick the two of you out of the meeting. And if I do that you won't get an invitation.

PEGGY: An invitation to what?

RAY: Shut up and you'll find out.
We're going to have a welcome home for John. The John J. Sullivan Welcome-Home Party, to welcome back our popular leader. I talked to some of the higher-ups in The Hall, and they're all in favor of it, every one I talked to.

FRANK: Tammany Hall?

RAY: What other Hall do I mean when I say The Hall?

FRANK: They going to have the party there?

RAY: No. We're going to have it somewhere around here. There's plenty of places we can have it right here in our own district. And that's what they want over at The Hall.
Give a party for John to show what his own people think of him.

TWO BY O'HARA

His own neighborhood. A demonstration to show that irregardless of him doing a stretch up the river, we still stand by him. We want a big turnout. We want to show the whole world how we feel about John J. Sullivan, our loyalty to John in spite of the bum rap they hung on him.

TONY: What bum rap was that, Ray?

RAY: The rap he just got finished serving the time for.

TONY: He pleaded guilty.

RAY: He pleaded guilty to shield others higher up.

TONY: He did?

RAY: Everybody *knows* he did. The whole thing was a miscarriage of justice. John pleaded guilty to taking a $2500 bribe. What's $2500 to John J. Sullivan, I ask you? Chicken feed. But that's all they could pin on him. The reform element had to have a fall guy so they could look good, and John was it. Everybody knows about that deal.

TONY: Well, are those higher-up guys gonna pay for this party?

RAY: Indirectly. Indirectly.

TONY: Indirectly is all right with me, Ray. Directly or indirectly, as long as they pay for it and I don't.

RAY: What they want over at The Hall is a good big turnout, a real sincere welcome to John---

TONY: That much they owe him, and no doubt about it.

RAY: And prove to those stiffnecked reformers that all right, they sent John to Sing Sing, but a lot of good it did them, because we all love him just the same as when he went up.

TONY: I look around this room and I don't see any of the big fellows from The Hall. Will they be there the night of the party?

RAY: Sure they will. Of course they will. But the welcome home is supposed to be started by John's friends, here in the district. We don't even want it to look as if it was started in the John J. Sullivan clubhouse. That's why you don't see any of the organization men here today. Just his close friends, his intimate associates that he more or less grew up with.

TONY: His dear old drunken mother, will she be at the party?

RAY: We'll have her there if she's in good enough shape. We won't have to keep her there very long.

PEGGY: What kind of a party is it going to be? A beefsteak?

RAY: No, more of a reception followed by dancing.

WILLIE: The booze'll be free?

RAY: Well sure.
   The tickets will be marked $5 apiece, but they'll be distributed free. Voluntary contributions by the businessmen, the storekeepers and the landlords.

TONY: Do you need any help selling ads for the program, Ray? You're printing a program, naturally?

RAY: Yes, I'm taking care of all that.

TONY: I kind of thought you would.

RAY: Yeah, and I kind of thought if anybody asked that question, you'd be the one, Tony. Don't I always take care of the programs?

TONY: That you do, Ray. But it's the kind of work I'd like to get into.

RAY: Well, if I ever need a helper I'll keep you in mind.
   Oh, there'll be something for everybody. For instance, Dick. We'll have a contract with Dick to furnish the music. Dick is all right with 8-0-2, aren't you, Dick?

DICK: Sure.

TONY: You jumped right over me, Ray. I was asking you about the program ads, and the next thing you're talking about a contract with Dick.

PEGGY: I'd like to get the checkroom.

WILLIE: Oh, no. I get the checkroom. That's for me and Mona.

PEGGY: You don't have no monopoly on the checkroom. And anyway, your sister's gonna be too busy that night to be stashing away hats and coats.

MONA: Let her have the checkroom, Willie.

WILLIE: You say let her have the checkroom. That's all right for you, if you want to give it up, but don't you speak for me. That's a nice buck at a party like this. How many'd you figure'll turn out, Ray?

RAY: Five hundred invitations, but there should be a thousand there.

WILLIE: That's two-fifty, figuring a quarter apiece. There's always some dimes, and some skulls that don't leave no tip at all, but these kind of parties you often get a buck. It comes to around a quarter each.

PEGGY: I'll be satisfied with half of that.

WILLIE: I'll pay you $25 and I won't search you, or I'll pay you fifty but that means a search.

PEGGY: I wouldn't let you put your paws on me.

WILLIE: Believe me, Peggy, I consider I'm paying myself $25 to put my paws on you.

SPIDER: I'd like to have the crap game. If I can have the crap game from ten o'clock to when you break up, that's all I want.

RAY: That, and the key to the United States Mint.

SPIDER: Well, you got the program ads. Willie got the checkroom. We're all entitled to something.

Far From Heaven

FRANK: I thought this was a welcome home for John. It's turning into a grafter's picnic.

RAY: We didn't get around to you, yet, Frank.

PEGGY: Yeah, listen to The Altar Boy.

FRANK: I don't want anything. I don't want a thing.

RAY: You never want anything, Frank. But you always want to sit next to the guest of honor. I never knew it to fail. You always make a holy face while the boys are cutting up the contracts. You don't want a thing. But if anybody wants to shake hands with the guest of honor they have to push you out of the way first. "Who's that sitting next to John J. Sullivan? Why that's Francis Xavier Gaffney, of Gaffney & Gaffney, insurance dealers."

FRANK: What's wrong with that?

RAY: Nothing wrong with it, nothing at all. But don't look down your nose at the rest of us, Frank. You get yours in free advertising.

FRANK: It's not so free, let me tell you.

RAY: We got some late arrivals.

(*As three men enter. They are:* BRENDAN DOUGHERTY, EDGAR ST. JOHN, *and* STITCH O'HEARN. *Those already present greet the newcomers by name.*)

RAY: Brendan. Edgar. Stitch. Have a seat.

BRENDAN DOUGHERTY: Before I sit down, I want to put in for the flowers.

RAY: What flowers?

BRENDAN: I hear you're having a beefsteak for John Sullivan. Well, nobody else gets the flower contract, you understand that.

RAY: We're not having a beefsteak for John.

BRENDAN: Well whatever it is you're having. You'll want flowers, and don't you give it to one of those Greeks. (*Addressing the assemblage*): I'm getting sick and tired of all of you. The last three funerals I went to I counted fifteen different floral arrangements that I happen to know came from those Greeks. I know because I checked. What did any Greek ever do for you?

SPIDER: He charges about half what you charge.

BRENDAN: Oh, you, Spider Rattigan. You don't count. You shoot crap with them so much you're beginning to look like one.

RAY: Sit down, Brendan. You're interrupting a meeting.

EDGAR ST. JOHN: May I ask if Brendan is correct? *Is* this meeting concerned with a beefsteak for John J.?

RAY: Yes, a party, but not a beefsteak. It's gonna be a reception followed by dancing.

EDGAR: Soup and fish?

RAY: Semi-formal. Those that have a Tux can wear them, and those that don't, don't have to. It's supposed to be a welcome home for John.

STITCH O'HEARN: Well, then do it right, why don't you? Make it formal. How many people you got coming?

RAY: Five hundred invitations, but it ought to run up to a thousand.

STITCH: A thousand? If I only rented a hundred Tuxes that'd be $300 for me. What do you think I'm in business for, my health? If you say semi-formal on the invitations, a lot of cheap bastards will use that for an excuse. "It didn't say formal on the invitation, so why should I rent a Tux?" But if you say formal, the women are going to make the men hire a Tux. Make it formal.

RAY: Some can't afford the $3.

STITCH: How much do the tickets cost?

Far From Heaven

RAY: They'll sell for $5, but most of them are going to be given away free.

STITCH: Then God damn it, make them pay for a Tux. Who got what so far? You got the program ads, Ray, I'll bet anything. Willie Devlin and Mona got the checkroom. Dick Sheridan's here, so I guess he got the orchestra contract. And I see Spider over there. You bringing a pair of dice, Spider? . . . What am I, a Jew or something? I want mine, just the same as everybody else.

Who's putting up the money? The Hall?

RAY: Some of it.

EDGAR: The Hall is putting up the money? That's interesting. Is this supposed to be a test of John's popularity?

RAY: Something on that order.

EDGAR: They want to see if his popularity survived his stretch in durance vile, is that it?

RAY: More or less.

EDGAR: Well, I have to take my hat off to the gentlemen at The Hall. Once again they command my respectful admiration. A master stroke. If the reception's a failure, our esteemed Leader will have been repudiated by his friends and neighbors, not by The Hall itself. If the reception on the other hand is a huge success, the gentlemen from The Hall will be right here among us, taking bows for their loyalty to our esteemed leader.

SPIDER: I never know when Edgar's sarcastic.

TONY: All the time.

EDGAR: You misjudge me, Anthony Flanagan.

TONY: Oh, no. No-no-no.

SPIDER: A reformer at heart, that's what you are, Edgar. Edgar St. John. With a name like that you can't be anything else. You ought

TWO BY O'HARA

to be with the Protestants with that name.

EDGAR: The St. Johns were members of the Church when the Rattigans and in fact all you Irish were pagans, centuries before you came to England and kidnaped young Patrick.

TONY: Here we go again.

EDGAR: No, I shan't waste my time trying to teach history to Spider Rattigan. But you Irish get nowhere when you say you were Christians before we were. Just happens not to be the truth, old boy.

TONY: My motto is, never talk religion or politics. Ha ha ha ha ha.

EDGAR: A good rule to follow, if you care nothing about conversation.

RAY: Edgar, you're so sarcastic, you don't know when Tony's sarcastic. Maybe Tony doesn't have your vocabulary, but he can be as sarcastic as any son of a bitch I ever knew.

TONY: Thank you, Ray. I'm sure you intended that for a compliment.

RAY: I did. And now let's get back to the main subject.

TONY: Religion and politics.

RAY: Politics. Because that's what we're here for. We're all John's best and closest friends here, and all the time he was in jail we could never get a thing, because we weren't organized. Our leader was doing time, we were disorganized, and we didn't count for anything over at The Hall. Any time any of us went over and asked for something, we didn't have anybody to speak for us. The big shots at The Hall would stall us off. We didn't have anybody to take John's place---

PEGGY: You tried.

RAY: I tried to fill in while he was away, but with no intention of sneaking in as leader. I'm not the politician John J. Sullivan was or is, and I know it. I'm better off where I am. As a police reporter I'm one of the best, but I don't have what it takes to be a real politician. You're either born with it or you're not. So I only filled in for John.

But now listen to me, all of you. If we put on a good show for John, we'll have him back on his two feet inside of a couple weeks, and everybody in this room, everybody on the Welcome Committee stands to benefit.

TONY: That's right, Ray. You're no politician.

You think like one, but then you have to go ahead and tell everybody what you're thinking.

Well, I'm willing to put on a good show for John.

SPIDER: So am I.

OTHERS: So am I. So am I. We all are.

EDGAR: You all realize, of course, that the men at The Hall are perfectly well aware of this meeting and everybody that's present. You also realize that if the welcome-home party is a flop, not one of us here will ever again get anything from The Hall. Not a thing. Not even to fix a parking ticket.

WILLIE: I don't have a car.

EDGAR: Willie reduces everything to the basic essentials.

RAY: Yeah. Well, wuddia say we start with where we're gonna have this thing. Who has any suggestions?

(*At this moment the door opens and a large man stands framed in the doorway. He is almost foppishly dressed, and he is fully conscious of the dramatic effect he creates by standing in the doorway; for he is* JOHN J. SULLIVAN, *and all the others in the room are stunned to see him. They wait in silence for his first words---will they be pleasant or will they be bitter? And he makes them wait, giving no*

TWO BY O'HARA

hint by his facial expression. Then he speaks):

JOHN J. SULLIVAN (*slowly smiling*): God bless all here.

(*Immediately they put up a cheer and start to crowd around him, shake his hands, touch him.*)

VOICES IN THE CROWD: John, John! Welcome home, John! God bless you, John. John J. Sullivan. You look like a million dollars. Our John. Good old John. Welcome home. God bless ya. Hurray for John J. Sullivan. Hurray for John!

(SULLIVAN, *accepting their homage, slowly moves inside the room, and he is followed by a pretty woman, thirtyish, possibly younger, loaded with sex and relying entirely on it for her self-assurance. The others, except* MONA DEVLIN, *barely notice her in their eagerness to paw* JOHN. JOHN *looks just once at* MONA, *then ignores her.* JOHN *eases his way to the spot that has been occupied by* RAY, *and* RAY *moves to the other side of the table, thus joining the others and leaving* JOHN *in the principal position. It is a subtle shift on the part of both men, but plainly shows who is in command.* JOHN, *with a slight gesture of one hand, puts an end to the demonstration and wordlessly orders the group to sit down. He points a finger to a chair at his right but somewhat removed, and the girl sits down and faces the others.*)

JOHN (*remains standing*): The old gang.
                        (*They applaud.*)
The old reliables.
                        (*They murmur appreciatively.*)
My real pals.
                        (*They applaud.*)
Well, you never saw the time when I was at a loss for words. (*He

is interrupted by laughter.) And the last eighteen months I been storing up a couple million of them. The State of New York very kindly, very considerately gave me the opportunity to rest my voice (*boos for the State of New York*). Some people used to say I talked too much. But on the other hand, on the other hand, there's a lot of people that I won't mention their names, but they're thanking the good Lord I knew when to keep my big mouth shut. Or else I would have had company up there where I just came from (*more boos*). There's a lot of people that had their usual Sunday dinners at Cavanaugh's, a lot of people that went up to the Polo Grounds and watch our Giants, a lot of people could take a ride down the Bay to Sandy Hook, and even some that mingle with the Park Avenue set at the Stork Club---they couldn't of done any of those things if I didn't know when to keep my mouth shut (*applause and boos*). So, rather than deprive them of their Sunday dinners at Cavanaugh's, and the prize-fights and all those other simple pleasures of life such as the Stork Club---I kept my mouth shut. I never said a word. The only word I said was when His Honor Judge Theodore M. Van Rhinebeck said "Do you plead guilty or not guilty," I said the one word, guilty, and you could hear a sigh of relief from the Criminal Courts Building all the way to the State Capitol in Albany. Good old John J. Sullivan kept his promise. He buttoned his lip and took the little train ride up the river all by himself, except for a pretty nice fellow named O'Shea, a detective sergeant, who kept telling me all the way he was only doing his duty. (*He laughs*.) I just remembered, I gave him a tip on a horse running at Bowie the next day, and I wonder if my horse came in.

Well, I'm glad to see my old pals here today. I came over here as soon as I heard about this meeting, so no use pretending I don't know what it's all about. And I appreciate it. Don't anybody think otherwise, because I do. I came over here first of all to say hello to each and every one of you, and secondly to tell you that this is all the welcome-home party I want. I mean that. I know that some of the gentlemen over at The Hall will put up the money for a big

TWO BY O'HARA

beefsteak or a reception, and I know Ray here'd do a hell of a good job. But I don't want it. I had all the publicity I want for the rest of my life. The next time I get my name in the paper is when it says Requiem High Mass at St. Anne's R. C. Church, kindly omit flowers.

BRENDAN: Don't put that in, kindly omit flowers.

JOHN: Well, they never pay any attention to that, Brendan. Anyway, give up the idea of giving me a welcome-home party. I'm going to stay out of the public eye. For the next few months I'm going to eat a lot of steaks and shad roe, and maybe have just a small liquid appetizer now and then. Smoke a good cigar. And go up the Polo Grounds and the Garden, take in a few shows, maybe get down to Hialeah and see if I can still hit a daily double once in a while. I'm going to live semi-retired. I happen to know this is the first meeting you had, so you don't have to change any plans, and I wanted to stop you before you went ahead. Just seeing you, my pals, all congregated here together with the best intentions, that's welcome home enough for me.

Now don't be disappointed, friends. I'm going to be around a long time and seeing a lot of you. I don't say I don't have any plans what to do with myself. There I'd be lying to you, and I save my lies for other people. But my plans call for no more publicity, living semi-retired, keeping my name out of the paper. If certain people begin to wonder what John J. Sullivan is up to, and they will--- they're not going to find out so easily, because I'm not going to be doing anything till I'm ready. I got a few cigar kewpons tucked away in an old wooden box, and some New Deal scrip, and maybe I'll have to get a paper route, but I got enough scratch to get by for a while. They slapped me in the can for eighteen months and some of them would like to slap me right back in again. But I got something all worked out and I'll be all right.

Now, you got any questions anybody?

SPIDER: Yeah. Who's the very beautiful stranger you didn't introduce us to.

Far From Heaven

JOHN: I was going to, Spider. And I might as well start with you. Alice, will you stand up a minute? Friends, this is Miss Alice Longford. Like the Spider says, the beautiful stranger.

(*polite applause*)

Alice hails originally from Pratt Falls, South Dakota. She was a society girl there.

ALICE LONGFORD (*standing*): Oh, come off it.

JOHN: She come East to seek her fortune.

ALICE (*to the others*): Don't believe everything he says.

JOHN: If any you playboys, like Dick, or Spider, or Tony---you think you reccanize Alice from The Paradise up on Broadway, that's a different Alice Longford.

ALICE: Sure is different now.

JOHN: This Alice Longford *resembles* that one.
   Aaah, you're all right, kid.

ALICE: Thanks.

JOHN: She don't mind a little ribbing, do you Cupcake?

ALICE: I don't mind a little.

JOHN: It's all for laughs. All for laughs.
   Now let me introduce you to my pals. This is Spider Rattigan, otherwise known as The Shortstop. You and him ought to have a lot in common because the Rattigans are in society too. Spider's old man used to be very high up in the Department of Sanitation. Up around Ninety-first Street, and that's pretty high. If you want to know what the Spider's old man did in the Sanitation Department, he wielded a wicked broom. And shovel. Andy Rattigan never disgraced the uniform, I'll say that for him. And he made a living following the horses, which is something I'd like to do though not in the same way. The Spider is a member of the

TWO BY O'HARA

sporting fraternity, as they say. That means he'll gamble on anything as long as he knows who's going to win. Then we have Brendan Dougherty. You'll see Brendan at all the weddings and funerals in the district, checking up on who got their flowers from the Greeks. You want to watch out for Brendan. He has a nasty temper. You get him angry and he's liable to clout you over the noggin with a dead carnation.

Edgar St. John, known as The Professor and also The Brain. Edgar teaches algebra and geometry over at Xavier's, on Sixteenth Street. That's why we call him The Professor. We go to him when we need advice on etiquette, like is it all right to wear brown shoes to a hanging. Edgar knows all the answers because his old man was a butler for Andrew Carnegie.

EDGAR: H. C. Frick.

JOHN: Watch your language, Edgar.

With Edgar is Stitch O'Hearn, one of our prominent business-men in the district, also known as The Priest. Where he got the name The Priest is he thought he had a vocation when he was around fifteen years of age, and he spent six months in a seminary. But somebody thought better of it. Whether it was the seminary people or Stitch I forget, but he came home and he's been with us ever since. Stitch is known as Stitch because his business is renting Tuxes and full dress for formal occasions.

Ray Fallon is our contact with the press. Ray covers Police Headquarters for the City News Association and dabbles in politics on the side. He knows every cop in New York City, including the Borough of Richmond. Staten Island. In fact, he knows the Staten Island cops very well because some of them he got sent there.

Dick Sheridan, plays saxophone with Tommy Dorsey, so he must be pretty good. Dick and I went to school together up to the eighth grade and then his uncle died and all he left was a saxophone and Dick's old man said, "Here, learn to play this God damn thing." The neighbors complained, but what if the uncle left a bass drum?

Far From Heaven

The Altar Boy. That's Frank Gaffney. You take one look at Frank and what else could you call him? He looked like an altar boy when he *was* an altar boy, and he looked like one ever since. But looks are sometimes deceiving. Don't be fooled by that angelic appearance. Frank is dumb like a fox. He carries his own deck, and I guess Frank makes more legitimate moola than anybody else in our crowd. Insurance business. Gaffney & Gaffney. The other Gaffney is his wife, and she's as smart as he is if not smarter.

Willie Devlin. We call him The Apostate. He was an altar boy too, the same time Frank was but not as long. They caught him swiping a bottle of altar wine and they kicked him off the altar. That's why they call him The Apostate.

WILLIE: Yeah. And who drank the wine with me?

JOHN: It tasted like vinegar. I never took a drink of wine since that I wasn't reminded of that time. You know that changed my mind about *me* having a vocation. My old lady wanted me to be a priest, but I couldn't drink that wine every day. Speaking of which, Ray, how about a couple quarts of whiskey for the prodigal son, and a bottle of the bubbly for Alice?

RAY: Right. What kind of whiskey?

JOHN: Well, let's start with any good rye, and some imported French champagne. Everybody else drink up, because I got those cigar kewpons.

As I was saying. The smiling gentleman over there is Tony Flanagan, also known as The Enforcer. I gave him that name. Ever since we were kids Tony was always the one that he'd start ribbing a guy and get him sore, and just about the time the guy was ready to take a poke at him, Tony'd start ribbing somebody else, and then before you knew it the two guys he was ribbing would get in a fight with one another. I guess I know Tony ever since he lived in the district and I never saw him in a fight. So I gave him the name of The Enforcer.

ALICE: Aren't you going to introduce me to the ladies?

TWO BY O'HARA

JOHN: Why sure I am. I'm saving the best for the last, like dessert. Peggy Moore, another society girl. She could of been in the Miss America contest when she was eighteen years of age, but that year they decided to have girls.

PEGGY (*not really angry*): Aah, shaddap, you big slob.

JOHN: I'm not kidding. Peggy was always one of the most popular debutantes in the district. I remember one time on Twenty-third Street she stopped a runaway.

PEGGY: Huh?

JOHN: There was this horse running away, endangering the lives of women and children and defying all the efforts of the police. But our Peggy ran out in the street and the horse took one look at her and fell dead.

PEGGY: You son of a bitch. You dirty Irish bastard.

JOHN: Fell dead in his tracks. Why they should of given Peggy a Carnegie medal, but you know what they did? They pulled her in for obstructing traffic. You see why I say there's no justice in this world?
And finally, Mona Devlin.

MONA (*rises*): I don't think you're so funny. I'm getting out of here.

> (*She stalks out.* JOHN *is surprised by the suddenness of the action but not by the action itself. The others look to see how he is taking the abrupt angry exit.*)

JOHN: Miss Devlin seems to have a fig up her ass.
Anybody know why?

WILLIE (*an unsubtle man*): I guess she thought---well, I don't know.

> (*He cannot help looking at* ALICE, *and his thought is the same as the others'.*)

JOHN: It's no way for an old pal to behave. I got nothing against her.

Well, come on, let's get to work on that booze. Alice, wudder you doing sitting there out of my reach? Come here where I can grab a handful.

(Curtain for End of Scene)

Act One
SCENE
2

Same as Scene 1, several hours later. All the players in Scene 1 are on stage, with the exception of MONA DEVLIN, *and all show some signs of the drinking.* JOHN J. SULLIVAN *is in his shirtsleeves, his collar open, no necktie, and one shirttail is hanging out. He has made himself comfortable, but he is nowhere near the limit of his drinking capacity. The jukebox is playing "The Dipsy Doodle," and* PEGGY MOORE *is dancing by herself.* BRENDAN DOUGHERTY *gets up to dance with her, but she refuses to dance with him and he goes off and dances by himself. They continue to dance after the music stops.* JOHN, *without a word, holds up a bill which is taken by* WILLIE, *who leaves to get nickels for the juke box.* TONY, *creeping under the table, is getting ready to give* STITCH *a hotfoot.* JOHN *watches the operation with a kind of benevolent malice.* FRANK GAFFNEY *is sound asleep sitting up in his chair.* SPIDER RATTIGAN, *quite drunk, has a hand on* ALICE's *shoulder, but she pays absolutely no attention to him or to his hand.* EDGAR ST. JOHN, *as good a drinker as* JOHN SULLIVAN, *is enjoying a newly lit cigar.* RAY FALLON, *seated at* JOHN's *left, is watching the*

proceedings as though trying to see it all through JOHN's *eyes.*
ALICE LONGFORD *is slightly bored, but keeps a hand on* JOHN's
shoulder so that he will not forget her. DICK SHERIDAN *in his chair
is eyeing her lecherously, if sleepily. He is trying to get her
attention, but he is easy to ignore.*

*In the silence that follows the end of the music the gathering
figuratively shake themselves, feeling the need for conversation.*

JOHN: Hey, Peggy.

PEGGY: What?

JOHN: I just had a great idea.

PEGGY: What?

JOHN: Why don't you and Brendan get married?

PEGGY: Marry Brendan? What for?

BRENDAN: Me marry Peggy?

JOHN: Sure. You'd make an ideal couple. Come on, come on. We'll
have a wedding.

PEGGY: Oh, you mean pretend?

JOHN: We'll have a black wedding, you know, have a black Mass.

BRENDAN: Not me. That's bad luck.

JOHN (*ignoring him*): We'll get Stitch to marry you---or I will. And
then we all get in a couple of hacks and go to some hotel. Rent the
bridal suite.

PEGGY: What for?

JOHN: I wanta see what'd be like, you and Brendan on your
wedding night. I'll give you fifty bucks.

PEGGY: Why does it have to be Brendan? You know what he is.

JOHN: That's why it's worth the fifty bucks.

Far From Heaven

BRENDAN: I should say not.

JOHN: Come on, Brendan, wuddia got to lose? I'll give you fifty bucks.

BRENDAN: I don't need it that bad.

JOHN: Did you ever have a woman, Brendan?

BRENDAN: That's none of your beeswax.

TONY (*who has finished the hotfoot*): I'll marry her for fifty bucks.

JOHN: You I know about. You'd marry anybody for fifty bucks, and anyway, you and Peggy been doing it since you were twelve years of age.

TONY: That was years ago. Years ago.

STITCH (*as the hotfoot takes effect*): Ow! Ow! My foot! God damn it. Who done that?

(TONY *points to* BRENDAN.)

The hell it was. I think it was you. These shoes cost me $14, you son of a bitch.

JOHN (*laughing, wets his thumb and peels off two bills which he tosses to* STITCH): Couple cigar kewpons. A tenner and a fiver.
  Spider, you're kind of rooty. How about you marrying Peggy?

SPIDER: Not me. Why don't you marry her?

JOHN: I got other plans.
  Edgar, how about you?

EDGAR: Without wishing to be ungallant, I must decline. But I'm curious, John. Tony volunteered and you refused his offer. Why Spider, and why me?

JOHN: Well, you want to know? Because Spider's getting himself all worked up over Alice, and you, because I got a hunch it's a long time since you had a piece.

TWO BY O'HARA

EDGAR: You mustn't always follow your hunches in such matters, John. However, thank you for your solicitude.

JOHN: Don't mention it.

EDGAR: Believe me, I won't.

JOHN: Well, Peggy, I did my best to accommodate you.

PEGGY: Well, thanks for nothin'. When I'm that hard up.

JOHN: What'll we do for a laugh? You know what I'd like to do, I'd like to turn in a fire alarm.

EDGAR: I advise against it.

JOHN: Oh, hell I'm not going to. But I was thinking of when I was a kid, some of the stuff we used to do. Stitch, wuddid we used to do for laughs?

STITCH: For laughs? Gee, I don't know. You mean against the law?

JOHN: Yeah. Like you and I, we turned in a couple false alarms.

STITCH: Break windows.

JOHN: Oh, hell, think of something good.

STITCH: Steal, you mean? The five and dime aint open now, unless maybe you go down to Fourteenth Street.

JOHN: I wasn't thinking of stealing.

STITCH: We could roll a sailor. You know, one of them foreigners off the boats.

JOHN: No.

STITCH: How about a sick call? You remember we used to put in a sick call. Get the priest to go to somebody's house, the old lady was dying?

JOHN: Yeah, and I got caught doing that. What was the name of that priest, he got me out of school the next day and beat the hell out of me with a belt.

Far From Heaven

STITCH: Was that Father Fogarty?

JOHN: Fogarty, that's right. How could I ever forget that name? I told him if he took off his collar I'd kill him, and the son of a bitch took off his collar and beat me some more. What ever happened to him?

STITCH: Oh, the last I heard he was up in Harlem somewhere. Maybe he's dead by now. He was an old man then.

JOHN: I had bruises on me for a week. Welts an inch thick. Peggy, what did we used to do?

PEGGY: Huh. You're askin' me?

JOHN: I don't mean bangin'. I mean before, when you were maybe ten, eleven.

PEGGY: Oh. Well, cut clotheslines.

JOHN: No.
    Spider, you remember the time we unhitched your uncle's horse. Took him right out of the shafts while your uncle was in getting a beer at Reardon's.

SPIDER: Yeah, I remember that. Only it wasn't my uncle's horse.

JOHN: For fifty bucks it was your uncle's horse.

SPIDER: Well, I won't bet you, but I know it wasn't my uncle's. It was my uncle's brother, had a bakery on Tenth Avenue. That's whose horse it was.

JOHN: Who was it poisoned Jimmy Brady's pigeons? Did they ever find out? This guy Brady was a man about twenty-five and he kept must-have-been fifty pigeons on the roof of his tenement where he lived. One day somebody fed them all rat poison and didn't Brady shoot somebody?

SPIDER: He sure did. He shot him good. He went to the chair for it. And he shot the wrong guy.

JOHN: Did they ever find out who did poison them?

TWO BY O'HARA

SPIDER: No, but it wasn't the guy Brady killed.

ALICE (*to* JOHN): Did you poison the pigeons?

JOHN (*shaking his head*): No, not me. I used to like pigeons. I wouldn't of poisoned a pigeon. I didn't like Brady, but I wouldn't of poisoned one of his pigeons. I think it was probably a woman. Women go for poison, not men.

ALICE: I like that.

PEGGY: Yeah, what's this women go for poison? It was in the paper where some guy in England poisoned ten or twenty people. That was no woman. It was some jerk guy.

JOHN: That was England.

EDGAR: I was wondering if you'd let that opportunity pass.

BRENDAN: Poison's no worse than a gun or a dagger. At least some poisons are painless. You can get rid of an enemy that way and you don't have to see them suffer.

ALICE: If I hated a person that much I wouldn't mind seeing them suffer.

BRENDAN: Well, I would.

TONY: I don't mind seeing them suffer. I just put a Mickey in your drink, Brendan.

BRENDAN: You did not. Did you? Did he? Did anybody see him put anything in my drink?

JOHN: I don't think it was a Mickey. I think it was just a pinch of salt. Does your drink taste salty?

BRENDAN: *I'm* not going to taste it now. Do you think I'm crazy?

(*In a byplay* TONY *shakes his head so that* JOHN *knows there is nothing in the drink.*)

JOHN: Here, let me taste it. Mickeys don't have any effect on me.

Far From Heaven

(*He downs the drink, smacks his lips.*) That wasn't salt. That was a real Mickey. I know the taste.

BRENDAN: And it won't make you sick? What is a Mickey, anyway?

JOHN: It's just a slug of croton oil. They give it to constipated cows.

BRENDAN: You must have a powerful constitution, that's all I'll say.

JOHN (*pointing with thumb to* ALICE): Ask *her* if I have a powerful constitution.

BRENDAN: I wasn't thinking of that way.

JOHN: What way?

BRENDAN: Well, the way you meant.

JOHN: What way did I mean?
   You know, Brendan, I think you got a dirty mind. I do. You know what I have a notion? I have a notion we ought to tie you up and marry you to Peggy anyway.

BRENDAN: Don't you dare! Don't you touch me.

JOHN: Get some of these dirty thoughts out of your head (*winks at* PEGGY). Peggy, will you marry him?

PEGGY (*playing along*): Well, if it'll get the dirty thoughts out of his head.

JOHN: And at the same time make a man out of him. Tony, you and Spider go see if you can find a rope. A piece of clothesline'll do.

BRENDAN (*frantic*): Don't you dare!

   (*Suddenly he dashes out of the room, and they all laugh.*)

JOHN: Ah, well, he gave us a laugh. And Brendan's not a bad fellow. Where I just come from I seen a lot worse, and some of them weren't that way when they went in.

TWO BY O'HARA

TONY: How about you, John? Did you make any new, uh, friends up there?

JOHN: Well, I tell you, Tony. It gets pretty lonesome up there. And like the fellow says, the only game in town.

ALICE: I'd be ashamed to admit it.

JOHN: Honey, I aint ashamed of anything.

(He is so earnest, so serious, that they all look at him in some surprise.)

JOHN: They sent me up there to put shame in me. Well, they didn't succeed, the lousy four-flushing bastards.

EDGAR: Are you speaking now of the people who let you down, or the reformers?

JOHN: I'm speaking of every son of a bitch that helped to put me in a cell. But don't worry about old John J. The one thing I learned how to do up there was wait. I learned patience, and I got a few cigar kewpons in an old wooden box.

(He suddenly turns violently on ALICE.)

Wuddia mean, you'd be ashamed to admit it?

(He kisses her roughly and paws her as the Curtain descends for End of Scene.)

Far From Heaven

Act One
SCENE
3

The Scene is a furnished apartment in London Terrace, the Time is the day following the preceding Scenes. The furniture is the kind chosen by a decorator working within a budget, modern but not tubular modernistic, and there is nothing of a personal nature, such as photographs, to make it really attractive.

JOHN J. SULLIVAN *in a Sulka-type dressing gown, is eating his breakfast and reading one of a stack of newspapers on the coffee table.*

JOHN (*He calls out*): Hey, Alice. Will you bring me my other glasses?

ALICE (*from bedroom*): Where are they?

JOHN: Somewhere in there. Look on top of the bureau. No, look in my suit I wore yesterday.

(*He removes the present glasses and she enters, bringing his glasses. She is wearing a print dress.*)

JOHN: Thanks.
I might as well throw these away. I see just as good without them. You want a paper. Which one d'you want?

ALICE: I want to read Dick Tracy.

JOHN: The *News.* Here y'are.
You ate, didn't you?

ALICE: I had a cup of coffee.

JOHN: There's more here if you want another cup.

ALICE: Not right away.

TWO BY O'HARA

JOHN: Take it now, or I'll drink it all.
That's one of the things I missed. A good cuppa coffee.

ALICE: Huh?

(*She is busy with the newspaper.*)

JOHN: Nothing.
You want to take in a show tonight?

ALICE: Huh? Oh, a show? Sure. Why not. What's good?

JOHN: Well, you got the paper. You pick out a show and I'll call George Faro. George can always get you anything the last minute. The biggest hits in town. Not saying he don't charge for them. Oh-ho-ho. And last minute fight tickets. Real ringside.

ALICE (*putting down the paper*): Yeah, I'd like to go to a show. What time is it?

JOHN: Uh---twenty of four.

ALICE: I guess it's too late for me to get an appointment at the beauty parlor.

JOHN: Only twenty of four. What time do they close?

ALICE: Oh, Derek won't take anybody after five o'clock. Unless you pay him double.

JOHN: Well, pay him double.

ALICE: I don't know.

JOHN: What *is* double?

ALICE: That all depends on what you want done. Are we going any place after?

JOHN: Well I don't see why not. Why is tonight an exception?

ALICE: Where are we going?

JOHN: I don't know. We'll hit a few spots. Anywhere you want to

Far From Heaven

go. We been to most of them since I got out, and I got a tendency to go to the same places. I get four-five places I like to check in every night.

ALICE: When are we gonna get all dressed up?

JOHN: When my new Tux is ready, in about two weeks.

ALICE: I never saw you in a Tux.

JOHN: I look pretty good in one. I took off a lot of weight but I still got too much lard on me to wear a double-breasted. I gotta start playing a little handball and working out. I'm in pretty good condition. Pretty good. But prison food, you know. They fill your belly and that's about all. I'm a pretty big eater, but you take notice I go for steaks and roast beef, and that don't put it on you as much as those fattening foods. If I had my choice of one thing to eat the rest of my life, only one thing, it'd be a steak. That's if I had to. Being's I don't have to, I'll eat a shad roe or once in a while a roast duckling. Although if you get me in an Italian place where they serve good spaghetti, I don't promise you I won't eat a gallon of that.

Did the phone ring while I was asleep?

ALICE: No, or if it did I didn't hear it.

JOHN: I gotta have another phone put in. This here's an unlisted number but I already give it to a few people and pretty soon they'll all have it. But I'm gonna have another phone that I won't tell anybody the number. You like this apartment?

ALICE (*looking around*): Sure. I guess it's all right.

JOHN: My brother Joe got it for me. Two-fifty I'm paying. That's fully furnished and maid service. When I get around to it I'll have a little contract with one of the hotels uptown. Then we don't have to come down here every night, if we don't feel like it. I always had a room or a couple rooms at the Astor, the Manger, the Taft. You want to go somewhere private and you don't want to come all the way down here.

TWO BY O'HARA

ALICE: Or take a woman.

JOHN: Well? Sure.

ALICE: You figure on having me move all my stuff in here?

JOHN: Why, sure. I thought that was all settled.

ALICE: Just move my stuff in, is that it?

JOHN: Well, I don't know what else you mean, Alice. You got no illusions about matrimony.

ALICE: *I* don't, but you do.

JOHN: When did I say anything about veiling up? I don't even know if you're single.

ALICE: I'm half. I'm separated.

JOHN: Well, that's what I thought. Listen, kid, I didn't ask you a lot of questions. I leveled with you. I'm a guy just out of stir, and I went for you but big. But getting married is the farthest thing from my intentions. If I gave you some other impressions, like you and I getting married, I don't know what I said to give you that impression.

ALICE: Well, I couldn't marry you right away.

JOHN: Oh, if you're thinking of five or ten years from now, maybe it'll work out that way. But I'm sorry if you thought it would be any sooner. I'm absolutely on the level with you about this. You want to check out, why I'd be sorry to see you go, but I wouldn't try to stop you. I played the field all my life, and I'm past forty now.
  Maybe it's a good thing we had this little talk, huh?

ALICE: I guess so.

JOHN: Yeah. So there won't be any misunderstanding. Like you take for example right after Christmas I gotta be out of town for two-three months. Well, what the hell, I wouldn't ask you to hang around doing nothing while I was away. I got a couple things cooking now that any one of them comes through and I'll have to be thousands of miles away. Not even in this country.

ALICE: You gonna give up politics?

JOHN: I didn't *say* that, honey. You mean because I expect to be out of town? Well, I have reasons for staying here and I have reasons for going away. You want to leave it at that?

ALICE: Whatever you say.

JOHN: When I get back, say March or April, if you didn't find somebody you like better, and *I* didn't, why what's to stop us from picking up where we left off? But we gotta keep it on a strictly for laughs basis, kid. Then you won't say I didn't give you a fair shake.

ALICE: I guess I *will* call Derek.
   Are you coming uptown with me?

JOHN (*relieved*): No, we don't go to the same beauty parlor. I tell you what you do, in my wallet, take a couple of those cigar kewpons marked one-hundred.

ALICE: You want me to? You gave me a hundred yesterday.

JOHN: I know I did. And maybe I'll give you one tomorrow. That's not a promise, not a real contract, but Daddy gave me a graduation present.

ALICE: Your father? I thought he was dead.

JOHN: Daddy isn't my father. That's more or less what you call a figure of speech. In other words, I had some dough waiting for me when I got out.

ALICE: Some of those bastards you took the rap for?

JOHN: Honey, it's all right to listen, but it's not a good idea to repeat what you hear. Unless you repeat it to me.

ALICE: I wouldn't be alive today if I repeated everything I heard.

JOHN: I more or less figured you that way.

TWO BY O'HARA

ALICE: You didn't only figure me that way. You asked the maitre-dee, you asked the press agent, and two of the girls in the line. And What's His Name the detective.

JOHN: You're too smart, but I don't like a dumb dame.

(*He reaches out, but she eludes him.*)

ALICE: Save it.

JOHN: Okay.

(*She goes to the bedroom, the door of which is at Left. He puts on his glasses and picks up a newspaper but is restless and walks up and down. She comes out of the bedroom, wearing white gloves and a hat.*)

JOHN: That was quick.

ALICE: I didn't phone him. I'm going right up. Where will I meet you?

JOHN: Dinty Moore's, ha' past seven. What show do you want to see?

ALICE: You pick one.

(*She leaves. As soon as he is sure she has gone he dials a number on the phone beside him.*)

JOHN (*high-pitching his voice*): Is Tony Flanagan there?
When'd he leave?
Was Spider Rattigan with him?
Thanks.

(*As he is talking the house phone rings.*)

Yeah?
All right. Tell them they can come up.

(*While waiting for them he clears the table of breakfast things except for one cup of coffee. As he finishes the buzzer sounds, and he admits* TONY *and* SPIDER *through door at Right.*)

JOHN: Hell-lo there fellows. Come right in. I didn't think you'd remember.

TONY: I didn't think you'd remember. You took on quite a bundle last night, John.

JOHN: Yes, I guess we all did. But I didn't forget asking you to drop in. Some other little things I just as soon draw the curtain, but that's neither here nor there.

Help yourselves. Over there. I think you'll find that bar pretty well stocked---unless you're looking for altar wine. Huh huh huh. It was sure good to see you fellows. Most of you.

(TONY *and* SPIDER *are helping themselves to highballs.*)

Say, what ever happened to Willie. I gave him a fi-dollar note to get nickels for the juke box, and that was the last I saw of him.

TONY: Willie is a little off his rocker.

JOHN: Oh, I didn't know that. When did that happen?

TONY: It's been coming on gradual-like.

JOHN: Oh? What's the trouble? Do they know?

TONY: We think he picked up a touch of big casino.

JOHN: The syph? Willie?

SPIDER: Well, you know Willie. If he can't get a job on shore, he ships out and he'll be away for a couple of months at a time. He has a seaman's ticket, so he can usually get a job as an A. B. or a deckhand.

JOHN: He was all right when they put me away.

SPIDER: No he wasn't. He was beginning to show it then. You didn't see him as much.

TWO BY O'HARA

JOHN: Show it, you mean the brain wasn't working?

TONY: It was never a great brain at best. He never graduated from eighth grade.

JOHN: Yeah, he had a clap when he was sixteen, but that's supposed to teach you a lesson.

TONY: Not him it didn't.

JOHN: Well, I'm sorry to hear that. He won't go to any doctor, I guess.

SPIDER: Not him.

JOHN: Did anybody ever get a look at his dong?

TONY: Not me.

SPIDER: Me either.

JOHN: Does Mona know he has it? I guess not.

TONY: It's hard to say. He don't live home no more. He had a fight with his old lady, he owed her a year's board and she kicked him out.

JOHN: Where does he live?

SPIDER: Got a room over on Eleventh Avenue. That fleabag run by that Turkish fellow.

JOHN: Armenian. Kallunian. Pete Kallunian. That was the voting address for when we brought in repeaters from The Bronx. Well, if Willie ever comes here I guess I hang a sign on my can, Out of Order.

Smoke a cigar? Help yourself to a pack of butts.

(continuing)

Tell you what was on my mind when I asked you to drop in. Now don't you repeat any of this. This is strictly under the hat. I got a couple of things lined up that I want to take a little time weighing the pros and cons. They all look pretty good now, but I don't want to rush into anything. I want to have a kind of vacation. Two years up the river, I'm entitled. And I got a few cigar kewpons salted away. So I'm in no hurry. But on the other hand, the way I spend it, you know I get rid of a buck very fast and I'm gonna reach down in my little wooden box and I'll get a handful of air, one of those days. So I'm doing a little thinking.

Either one of these propositions, I'm going to need a couple fellows I can trust, and you two naturally came to mind. I can't say the nature of these propositions. *You* have to trust *me*. But it won't be politics. On the other hand, it will be confidential work. Work of a confidential nature.

SPIDER: Is it somebody you met up the river?

JOHN: Well, now, Spider, that's where you have to trust me, because I'm not saying anything. Not a thing. Maybe you want out?

SPIDER: No, no. I don't want out, John. But if I'm in I want to know what I'm in.

JOHN: You're in the chips, is one thing. Steady pay and you don't have to give up anything you're doing now. You'll get your pay every week, and some weeks you won't hear from me except when I hand you your fifty bucks.

SPIDER: Fifty bucks a week?

JOHN: Every week you work for me. In advance. I'll start with your first week today, although I don't know when I'm gonna need you.

TONY: I'm here, John. Don't forget me.

JOHN: I won't forget you, Tony. I just want both of your confidence, and you can signify that by saying you want in.

TONY: I'm in.

SPIDER: So am I.

TWO BY O'HARA

JOHN: That's all I wanted to know. I got you here to find out if you liked my proposition.

TONY: Well, we don't know what the proposition is, but it looks good so far.

JOHN: It'll be confidential work.

SPIDER: Finding out stuff. Here in the district, I guess.

JOHN: Mostly, yes. Later on I may want you to take a trip once in a while.

TONY: I'll go anywhere, if I'm paid.

JOHN: You'll be paid, and you'll go first class. But that won't be for three or four months from now.

SPIDER: Will there be any rough stuff, John?

JOHN (*laughing*): Spider, you're always looking for a little action. No, no rough stuff. I don't say there won't ever be no rough stuff. But when that time comes I'll discuss it with you and naturally you'll get extra for that.

(*wets his thumb and takes wallet out of his dressing gown pocket*)

JOHN: You fellows when you come up here didn't know it was gonna be payday, but that's what it is. Fifty for you, Tony. Spider, fifty for you.

SPIDER and TONY: Thanks. Thanks, John. Thanks.

(*Each looks at his five ten-dollar bills, then puts the money in his pocket.*)

TONY: I like the idea of them trips. You know the farthest I was ever away from New York City and over in Jersey---Scranton P A, to one of my aunts' funeral. My mother's sister. I was around fifteen years of age.

JOHN: Well, I been a lot of places. Florida. Chicago. Philly. Kansas

Far From Heaven

City. Houston, Texas. I like to travel, too. I want to go to Paris. Paris, France, and get inside of a real French hookshop. They tell me, I met a guy up the river, and he said you can get anything there. I said you can get anything here in New York City, but when he started to tell me about some of the joints he went to in Paris! This con was a waiter, some kind of a Hungarian or Rumanian, worked in all the best hotels all over the world. Handsome fellow. Doing a bit for armed robbery, and he swore the cops planted the roscoe on him and for once I believed him. Too smooth an operator to get caught with a gun on him. He gave me a couple addresses if I ever go to Paris. But then you have to look at it the other way. I mean, well, Willie would have been better off if he didn't travel.

(They laugh.)

Say, speaking of Willie, makes me think of Mona again. Are she and Ray serious about getting married?

SPIDER: Well, that's what you hear.

TONY (*quickly*): I heard it but I don't believe it for a minute.

JOHN: Listen, it's all over between Monar and I, Tony. That was over before I went to the clink. You could see for yourself how she walked out yesterday. I was surprised to see her there at all, but I guess she wanted to get a look at my new beautiful baby doll Alice. She something, that Alice? I seen a picture of her in some magazine, and the night I got sprung I headed right for The Paradise.

(The buzzer sounds.)

Ehh. Who would that be? Oh, maybe Ray Fallon.

(*He goes to the house phone and while he is talking* TONY *says to* SPIDER): "You earned *your* fifty bucks, you dumb bastard. That's what he wanted to know."

JOHN (*on house phone*): Apartment 12-A.
Well, ask Mr. Fallon to come right up, please.

TWO BY O'HARA

(He hangs up and quickly speaks to the two men.)

You two fellows, go down the hall where it turns right. You wait there till Ray's inside here. I don't want him to see you. He isn't going to be in on our deal. Fast, fast. You'll hear from me.

(They exit hastily, and JOHN *removes signs of their visit. He admits* RAY.*)*

JOHN: The mighty Fallon. Come in, boy. Come in sit down and let's tell a few lies.

Whatever you want to drink, I think you'll find it there. I'm just having a little cold coffee.

(He shakes RAY's *hand and holds* RAY's *right elbow in his left hand.)*

RAY: You got quite a place here, John. I got a lot of friends living in the building but they don't have your view.

(He goes to the window and JOHN, *behind him, pantomimes the act of pushing him out.)*

JOHN: Yeah. The Palisades. And the big boats on the North River. No drink?

RAY: I'm on my way to work, John. If it's all the same to you.

JOHN: Hell, I don't believe in forcing a man to drink, not when a guy has a job to take care of.

I'm glad you could spare a minute. I wasn't sure you'd remember.

RAY: I wrote it down on a piece of paper.

JOHN: Excellent precaution. I guess that's your newspaper training.

Ray, I wanted to ask you. Do you think I done the right thing by calling off the welcome-home party?

RAY: That's hard to say, John. A lot of people'll be disappointed.

Far From Heaven

Friends want to show you what they think of you---

JOHN: Yeah, but that's what I was afraid of.

RAY: How do you mean, John?

JOHN: Well, if some of my so-called friends wanted to show me up, giving a party and staying away would just about do it, wouldn't it? Make a public horse's ass of me. Give a party for me, but get the word around that nobody's to show.

RAY: I don't think that was the way it was intended.

JOHN: Well, that's what I wanted to know. You're on the inside, and you can tell me what they had in mind.

RAY: You mean over at The Hall?
   Well, they were willing to spend the money for the party. They'd pick up the tab. But they were, I admit, sort of hesitant about sponsoring it. This district kind of fell apart when you were sent away. There was nobody to take your place.

JOHN: There was you, Ray.

RAY: I did the best I could, but I wouldn't quit my job, because you were coming back and where would I be if I quit my job? Maybe it isn't much of a job, but I've been there a long time, John. I know the political game all right, but I wasn't cut out to be a leader.

JOHN: Oh, you don't have to be so modest, Ray.

RAY: That's the truth. I'd go to the clubhouse and sit at your desk, but all I was was some kind of an errand boy between the clubhouse and The Hall.

JOHN: Why, I heard you were doing a hell of a job.

RAY: You couldn't have heard that, because it wasn't true.

JOHN: I heard it, though. I heard you were at the club every afternoon, or anyway most afternoons, and you always had somebody there nights. Maybe you didn't follow my system, Ray, but I hear they were getting used to your system.

RAY: How so?

JOHN: Well, *you* know. Every club in New York City, the people know the leader is there every night, but I understand you got them coming in the afternoons. Which is fine, Ray. Excellent. But what it shows, Ray, what it shows is that the people began thinking of you as their leader.

RAY: No, not with a big lifesize picture of you hanging in back of me.

JOHN: Oh, you left the picture hanging?

RAY: Why, sure.

JOHN: Well wuddia know about that?

RAY: It's there now. We never took it down. And they never changed the name of the club. It's still the John J. Sullivan Democratic Club. It was never anything else. You know that.

JOHN: I knew about the name. I didn't know about the picture.
    Well that leads me to my next question, Ray. What do you think about me going back into politics?

RAY: Hell, you were never out of it, at least as far as I was concerned.

JOHN: I didn't have no telephone in my cell, Ray. And maybe you noticed the last two years I didn't get down to many funerals. In fact, now I come to think of it, I saved a lot of money by not having to buy wedding presents.

RAY: You're telling me. Half of my salary from the club went for wedding presents.

JOHN: It's supposed to. You're not supposed to get rich off the salary the club pays you. You know what the most salary I ever got from the club was?

RAY: No.

Far From Heaven

JOHN: Seventy-fi dollars a week.

RAY: That's what they paid me.

JOHN: But you made out all right financially otherwise.

RAY: Nothing big.

JOHN: Ray, I want you to level with me. Who got the big stuff while I was away?

RAY: I don't know for sure, but I never saw any of it.

JOHN: This big garage they put up down on Tenth Avenue. They didn't see you about that?

RAY: Not a nickel.

JOHN: Hmm. Somebody at The Hall was bypassing you. Didn't you complain? You were entitled.

RAY: I complained, but I didn't get anywhere.

JOHN: They brushed you off?

RAY: Not exactly brushed me off. They said I didn't have it coming to me. They said---

JOHN: Who said?

RAY: The men over at The Hall. Reagan. Goldberg. Bert Ryan. They said you were costing a lot of money, and all the big stuff out of this district had to make up for what you were costing them.

JOHN: Well, I was the one that went to prison and I kept my lip buttoned up tight.
But didn't they say you'd get yours later?

RAY: Yeah, they said---

(*He stops abruptly and there is a silence between them as* JOHN *smiles at* RAY, *a very unpleasant smile.* JOHN *enjoys* RAY's *discomfort, lets him squirm.*)

TWO BY O'HARA

JOHN (*ever so kindly*): Go on, Ray. You were saying?

RAY: Well, they said, uh, they said I'd be taken care of.

JOHN (*snorting*): You want me to tell you what they really said, Ray? You want me to tell you, just like I was in the room at the time?

It was Bert Ryan, wasn't it? Yeah, it was Bert Ryan. And you know what he said? See if I'm right. Bert said, "Ray, you'll get yours when we get rid of John Sullivan. But first we gotta get rid of Sullivan." Is that what Bert said, Ray?

RAY: No. You got it all wrong.

JOHN: I got it all right, you mean. You miserable son of a bitch. You double-crossing, two-bit bastard. I had you pegged five years ago. Five years ago you went to Bert Ryan over my head, without consulting me, and you told Bert you wanted to run for State Assemblyman.

RAY: All right, what if I did?

JOHN: What if you did? You son of a bitch, behind my back you snuck over to Bert Ryan that hates my guts, and you knew he hated my guts, and you told him you wanted to run for State Assemblyman. But you got a no answer. Bert Ryan was afraid of me then. I was too big then. But I tell you what happened, in case you think I don't know. Mr. Bert Ryan had a meeting with Charley Reagan and Irving Goldberg and he told them, he said John Sullivan is having trouble keeping his fellows in line. He said Ray Fallon wants to run for assemblyman, with or without John Sullivan's consent.

That was the first time Mr. Bert Ryan got anything to use against me. You were the first one to put the knife in my back. It didn't go very deep, but you convinced Mr. Bert Ryan that it could be done.

From that time on I had more and more trouble with Mr. Bert Ryan, till finally it ended with me taking the rap and doing two years in Sing Sing. You know who really put me in Sing Sing, Ray?

You, you miserable double-crosser. How do you like that?

RAY: You're crazy.

JOHN: Oh, sure. Sure.

So who do they get to take my place while I'm up the river? Mr. Ray Fallon. Who is Ray Fallon? Some newspaper reporter, never had a political job in his life. Supposed to be John J. Sullivan's best friend. Only taking over the leadership till Sullivan gets out of jail.

Sure, I'm crazy.

Then what next? You and Mr. Bert Ryan decide to throw a welcome home for John J. Sullivan, the peerless leader and the great martyr. And boy are you gonna sabotodge that party?

RAY: Keep talking if it makes you feel any better.

JOHN: I'll keep talking and you'll keep listening, because I aint through.

Who do you pick to be on the welcome-home committee? My lifelong friends, sure. You don't think I never saw through that one. Why wasn't there one big political name on the committee? Because you and Mr. Bert Ryan made sure there wasn't. Who do you get? (*He starts ticking off with his fingers.*) You got a small-time hoodlum, Spider Rattigan. You got a fairy that runs a florist shop, Brendan Dougherty. You got Stitch O'Hearn that runs a secondhand clothing store. You got a saxophone player that smokes muggles, Dick Sheridan. Frank Gaffney, an insurance chiseler. Tony Flanagan, a cheap wisecracker. Edgar St. John, a stool pigeon for the guys over at The Hall. And who elsa you got? You got poor Peggy Moore, a hooker since she was sixteen years of age. You got Willie Devlin, feeble-minded from the syph. *And,* just for the hell of it, his sister Mona. Your two-timing girl friend.

That's my welcome-home committee. Temporary chairman, Mr. Ray Fallon, my oldest and dearest friend.

I'm crazy? Sure. You didn't think I knew about you and Mona? Why you moved in there before they had a chance to give me the jailbird's haircut. That's what was behind it all. You were always jealous of me with Mona. So you wanted to run for assemblyman, you wanted to be leader, you wanted to show Mona you were as good as me. And you done your little bit to get me put away, *out* of the way. And you moved right in with Mona. But I bet it kills you when you have to remember that I was there first, and I was there a thousand times ahead of you, Ray. Eas'ly a thousand times, me and Mona.

RAY (*rising*): Yeah. You're crazy. Stir crazy.

JOHN: Uh-huh. Ask the little lady about Asbury Park. Just say Asbury Park to her. You don't have to say anything else but those two words.

> (*He reaches forth and in an elaborate gesture takes a cigar out of the box in front of him, bites off the end and spits it on the floor as* RAY *heads for the door.* JOHN *does not look up until he hears the door close, whereupon he goes into a rage, breaks the cigar in two, and beats the table with both fists. Curtain for End of Scene.*)

Act One
SCENE
4

The apartment. Late that night. The apartment is dimly lighted. ALICE, *in the same print dress she wore earlier, is reading* Variety. *She gets bored with it and tosses it aside impatiently and gets up and looks out the window, but is not interested in the night view. She looks at her wristwatch under the floor lamp and decides to have something to eat. She crosses from R. to L., and while*

Far From Heaven

crossing looks, without stopping, at the sleeping figure of JOHN J. SULLIVAN *on the couch. She goes out of the room but returns immediately with a bottle of beer and a glass and a box of pretzels. She goes back to her chair, but in seating herself she moves the chair noisily and* JOHN *begins to wake up.*

He is in pretty bad shape and does not immediately know where he is until he sees ALICE.

JOHN: Oh, hyuh.

ALICE (*sore as hell*): Hello.

JOHN: Wuddia got there, a beer?

ALICE: That's what it looks like, doesn't it?

JOHN: Is it cold?

ALICE: It's cold.

> (*John scratches his head, stretches his stiff neck, and lights a cigarette.*)

JOHN: Time is it?

ALICE: Twenty-five after eleven.

JOHN: Twenty-five after eleven. Twenty-five after eleven. There any more beer out there?

ALICE: There's some more.

JOHN: How'd you like to bring me a bottle?

ALICE: Get it yourself, I'm not gonna wait on you. I did enough waiting for one night.

JOHN: Twenty-five after eleven.

> (*He gets to his feet, still wearing the Sulka dressing gown and his pajamas. He looks at her but decides not to cope with her anger. He yawns, then goes out and brings back a*

bottle of beer and a glass and pours some slowly and takes a sip.)

JOHN: Good and cold. Tastes good. Whatter you eatin'?

ALICE: A nice thick juicy steak with mushrooms.

JOHN: Pretzels? Throw me a couple, will you?

(She throws the box, hard. He puts up his hand to stop it, lets it fall, then takes out a couple of pretzels and has a bite of one.)

JOHN: How longa you been here?

ALICE: I've been here since a quarter after nine.

JOHN: How long did you wait at Moore's?

ALICE: Two stinkin' hours.

JOHN: Well, didn't you know anybody?

ALICE: I knew plenty, and they knew me, and you humiliated me, you lousy stinkin' heel.

JOHN: Why didn't you use the God damn phone?

ALICE: Because I didn't know the number and the operator wouldn't give it to me.

JOHN: So then you used your head and came down. Did you have your hair fixed? Yeah, you did. Looks good.

ALICE: Listen, how many times do you think you're gonna get away with this, humiliating me out in public?

JOHN: I never done it before, did I?

ALICE: You bet you never done it before. Well don't think you're ever gonna do it again. I thought maybe something happened to you, but when I get down here all you are is stinkin' lousy drunk as a pig, a bottle in one hand and another bottle spilt all over the floor. If I knew that was all you were I wouldn't of left Moore's. Plenty of fellows there wanted to take me out.

JOHN: What the hell, I'm gonna take you out.

ALICE: The condition you're in? You can't stand up.

JOHN: Then we'll go some place where I can sit down.

ALICE: I don't wanta be seen with you.

JOHN: Wuddia wanta do? Stay here and spend a quiet evening at home? I don't have any socks for you to darn. I got all new. I got everything new. I got new socks, I got new silk undies, I got six new suits of clothes, I got three dozen neckties. I got three new pair of shoes and six more on the way. And my Tux. My new Tux'll be ready in a couple weeks. I got everything brand new. I even had my chest waxed for you. So what more do you want? Tell you what I'll do. I'll take a shower and put some clothes on. Have a snort, and we'll go uptown. It's only a little after eleven, things are just getting started. This is the time I usually show up anyway. Tell you what I'll do. I'll take you to Moore's and then all your buddies'll see you with me and that way you save face. You wanta save face, like in China? All right, I'll take you to Moore's.

ALICE: Like hell you will.

JOHN: All right, then I won't. Just tell me what you'd rather do and we'll do it. But for God's sake, don't sit there like a God damn carbuncle ready to bust open. You're sore, and all right, you got a right to be sore, but don't louse up the whole evening. I'll make it up to you, but I aint gonna eat dirt for you. Not John Joseph Sullivan, kid. I go for you and I go big, but no discipline, kid. No schoolteacher act. No writing on the blackboard, I'm sorry, 500 times.

I got a load on, and I stood you up, and I apologize. That's as far as we go. That's where we get off. You want another beer, or a snort?

ALICE: No.

TWO BY O'HARA

JOHN: I'm gonna have a snort and then I'll take a shower. Who'd you see at Moore's? Anybody I know?

ALICE: I don't know who you know. Yes, I saw one fellow. Ryan?

JOHN: Which Ryan? You remember his first name? Bert Ryan?

ALICE: Yes, Bert. That's what they called him.

JOHN (*pouring a drink of whiskey*): How'd you happen to come in contact with *him*?

ALICE: He was with a fellow I know and they came over and sat down where I was.

JOHN: And how did my name crop up in the conversation?

ALICE: "Who're you waiting for?" the fellow said, the one I know, and I said I was waiting for you, did he know you. He didn't know you, but the other one did. Ryan.

JOHN: What'd you think of him---Ryan. On first impression.

ALICE: Well, I got a little sore at him.

JOHN: Why?

ALICE: Because as soon as I mentioned your name he put on a sarcastic look.

JOHN: What did he say? Did he say anything?

ALICE: Yeah. He said I oughta be able to do better than that, meaning you.

JOHN: And that made you sore.

ALICE: Well, a total stranger, he ought to wait and find out what is it with you and I, at least before he starts making cracks. Then when you didn't show up I got even sorer, at him and you and the whole God damn stinkin' lousy New York City. I hate this stinkin' town. I wish I was back in Detroit.

JOHN: You're a Polack, aren't you?

Far From Heaven

ALICE: And proud of it. I wish I never saw an Irishman or a Jew or a Wop or any of you.

JOHN: Well, we're all very glad to see *you*, Alice.

ALICE: Yeah, sure. My mother, forty-two years of age, looks better than your women.

JOHN: Maybe you can fix it up for me if I ever get out that way.

ALICE: My old man would pick you up like this and splash you against the wall. I got two brothers would cut your heart out for saying that about my mother. One of them did cut a fellow's heart out. If you don't believe it you can look in the papers. Ziggy Polowski.

JOHN: Then what happened to Ziggy?

ALICE: They got even with him. But I got my other brother still living.

JOHN (*the booze reviving him*): Well, I trust he lives to a ripe old age. And your father. And your mother. And all the Polowskis. What's the other brother's line of work?

ALICE: He works for Ford, or did the last I heard. Maybe he went to Cleveland. I don't know.

JOHN: Why would he go to Cleveland?

ALICE: To live with our cousins. He and the old man were always having fights. I don't know. Maybe he didn't *go* to Cleveland. Maybe he went to Chicago. Or maybe he's still working at Ford's.

JOHN: You're sort of out of touch with your family.

ALICE: I ran away.

JOHN: Why?

ALICE: None of your lousy stinkin' business why.
   That Ryan fellow, is he some kind of a big shot?

TWO BY O'HARA

JOHN: Why?

ALICE: Oh, I don't know. He didn't look like anything, but they all catered to him. But he didn't look like one of the mob. He's in your racket, huh?

JOHN: Very much so.

ALICE: You better get him out of it before he gets you out first.

JOHN: Alice, I wish I knew you ten years ago.

ALICE: When I was ten years old?

JOHN: No, but when *I* was *thirty*.

(Curtain for End of Scene)

Far From Heaven

Act Two
SCENE
1

JOHN's *apartment. Several weeks later. Afternoon.* JOHN *with a* Racing Form *and* Morning Telegraph *on the coffee table in front of him, has a pencil between his teeth and is frowning over a sheet of paper.* ALICE, *dressed for the street, awaits his words. He shakes his head.*

JOHN (*largely to himself*): It's gotta be the Whitney horse. I don't see any other horse in the race except maybe this God damn California horse, Winaway. The Whitney horse'll be pretty close to even money by post time. Now the age-old question, do I go with the favorite, or do I gamble with the California horse? He has a chance, this Winaway. He'll get a good ride from McArdle. The Whitney horse beat him once by two lengths but on a muddy track. In fact Winaway never lost to a bad horse. The only horses ever beat him were Stingeroo and My Chance and they're not in this race. Hell. When in doubt, don't play the favorite. I'm going for a C-note across the board. Winaway.

You made up your mind?

ALICE: The Whitney horse. Ten dollars across the board.

JOHN (*relieved*): Okay.

(*He dials a number.*)

Hello, this is Number 857. Who's this? Johnny?

I want a hundred dollars across the board on Winaway, the fifth race at Belmont. You got that? And I got another bet for you. Ten dollars across the board, same race, only this bet is on the Whitney horse. No, I'm not hedging. You oughta know me by this time.

(hangs up)

Hedging. Me?

I hate to tell you, Alice, but you just threw away $30. Well, maybe not thirty. You could collect the place money and the show money, but I got this feeling. I'm overdue. How long since I had a winner?

ALICE: You had two winners the day before yesterday.

JOHN: But they didn't pay much. They were both favorites. I mean a real winner. This California horse could easily get off at eight-to-one, nine-to-one. If I could have one ten-to-one shot come in, then that could very eas'ly be the start of a winning streak, Alice. You know twice in my life I won every race on the card. Of course that was at the track. We ought to start going to the track. I always have better luck at the track.

ALICE: Then why don't we? I like to go to the track. But you never get up early enough.

JOHN: I gotta be here in case I get a call from a fellow.

ALICE: Whoever he is, he sure is taking his time. Three weeks.

(The house phone rings.)

Maybe that's him.

JOHN *(shaking his head)*: He won't be calling on the house phone. Answer it, will you?

ALICE *(obliging)*: Hello.
. . . It's Spider Rattigan.

JOHN: All right.

ALICE *(into phone)*: All right.

(to JOHN)

What time'll I see you?

Far From Heaven

JOHN: You wanta make it around six?

ALICE: Where?

JOHN: Barberry Room?

ALICE: Okay. Are we gonna eat there?

JOHN: No, we don't wanna eat there. It's too dark. Maybe we'll take a ride over and eat in Brooklyn. Gage & Tollner's. We'll see.

ALICE: Well, it'll be a change from Moore's, but I bet I know where we end up. Moore's.

JOHN: I might cross you and take you to Gallagher's. So long, kid.

ALICE: Bye.

> (*The buzzer sounds for the apartment door.*)

Will I let him in?

JOHN: Sure.

ALICE (*goes to door*): Hello, Spider.

SPIDER: Oh, hyuh, Alice.

ALICE: I'm just leaving.

SPIDER: Well, so long.

> (*He gazes somewhat longingly at her behind as she closes the door.*)

Hello, John.

JOHN: Some day maybe you'll have one like that, Spider.

SPIDER: If you ever get tired of that one, let me know.

JOHN: That won't be for a while, yet.
Where's The Enforcer? It's payday for him, too.

SPIDER: Tony? Tony said it'd be all right if I picked up his money.

TWO BY O'HARA

JOHN: Oh, is that what he said? He must have something good going for him if he's too occupied to come around for his fifty bucks. Here's yours, but if Tony wants his, let him at least have the politeness to come in person.

SPIDER: Don't get sore, John. Maybe he figures you didn't want to see him.

JOHN: Why would he figure that? When I don't want to see him, believe me he'll be the first one to know it. What is he, lushing it up some place?

SPIDER: No. I left him playing pool.

JOHN: Is that so? Who was he playing pool with?

SPIDER: I think maybe, let me think now. Him, and Stitch, and Willie Devlin.

JOHN: And somebody else. The somebody else wouldn't be Ray Fallon?

SPIDER: Ray. That's who the other one was. Ray took my cue when I dropped out. On the way over I kind of figured maybe you wanted Tony to find out something from Ray.

JOHN: Well, I didn't. Ray Fallon isn't confiding in Tony Flanagan. At least I don't think he is. What do you think, Spider?

SPIDER: Christ, I don't have the slightest idea.

JOHN: Do you think I can trust Tony?

SPIDER: Tony? Can you trust Tony Flanagan? Well, he's a friend of yours, and he got a contract with you.

JOHN: Supposing Ray offered him fifty-five a week over my fifty? Make it sixty. What would Tony do if Ray offered him sixty a week?

SPIDER: Why, I guess he'd come and tell you Ray was offering him sixty.

Far From Heaven

JOHN: You don't think he'd just take the sixty without telling me? That'd be a hundred and ten a week, a hell of a lot more than Tony's ever used to. And don't forget, Ray's in, and I'm out.

SPIDER: Yeah. Ray's in, and you're out. But that could be different. You got something big coming up and maybe it'll be bigger than what Ray has.

JOHN: And you're willing to go along with me?

SPIDER: Yeah, for a while anyway. See, John, I been in the chips bigger than Tony ever was. You know, I had thirty-four fights, one in the Garden, before I retired. Tony never had that kind of money. Not to mention, up till a few years ago I had a very good connection that I got very good money, even if it wasn't steady.

JOHN: Yeah, Spider. I understand you made a couple very big dollars. Out of town.

SPIDER: Oh, sure. Always out of town, John.

JOHN: Well, in town or out of town, you know what it feels like to be in the chips and Tony never did.

SPIDER: I aint saying don't trust Tony. But the fellow that never had any big money is liable to be greedy where money is concerned. I'm greedy, sure, but for me it won't be the first time, you know what I mean?

JOHN: I appreciate that, what you're trying to tell me. And we don't have to say no more about it.

SPIDER: Yeah, I don't want to say too much. I may be all wrong about Tony. You and him were always pals.

JOHN: I just wish the guy he stood me up for was somebody else, not Ray Fallon. That don't look so good. I guess it's all over town about me and Ray having a bit of a tiff.

SPIDER: It's around.

JOHN: What I don't like is Ray putting out some story that I was

sore on account of Mona. You know, in politics you got plenty of
things to differ on, but Ray's putting out this story that I have it in
for him because he moved in on Mona as soon as I got thrown in
the clink.

Can you picture me sitting up there in Sing Sing carrying a torch
for Mona? Me? I knew Mona upside down and inside out, and she's
still a good-lookin' broad, but all the time I was bangin' her I had
other dames and that made her sore as hell. I used to say to her,
"Listen, there's some guys can be satisfied with one woman, only I
don't happen to be one of them." I said I had no objection if she
wanted to two-time me, because I didn't consider it two-timing.
Two-timing is if you're married or gonna get married. But the
trouble with Mona, she wanted me to marry her and she wouldn't
take on another guy for fear I'd have a good excuse. But as soon as I
got put away she showed her true nature. She liked her nooky.
Oho, did she? And inside of a couple weeks she was in the hay with
Ray Fallon. I heard about it right away, but I never let on.

When I got out did I come rushing down here to raise hell with
her, or take a poke at Ray? Hell, I was out a week before I ever
showed in the district. And when I showed I had a broad with me,
Alice, that you gotta admit, she puts Mona Devlin in the shade.

SPIDER: Yeah, there's no comparison.

JOHN: There's absolutely no comparison. Alice is young, she got a
built on her, and if I told you the name of the guy I took her away
from, you'd run home and hide. You'd be afraid to know. Now
that's a broad I *would* think of getting married to, if I ever thought
of getting married to anybody.

SPIDER: Is she a Catholic?

JOHN: Well, yeah. She's Polack, but they're all Catholics.

So the story Ray Fallon's putting out is a lot of crap. I told him
off but good, but it wasn't over any dame. And I wouldn't curtail an
old friendship over any Mona Devlin, for God's sake. Ray's putting
out that story to cover up the real reason why I told him off.

You want to know the real reason, Ray Fallon is a dirty double-crossing son of a bitch from way back, not just the eighteen months I was in stir.

SPIDER: Well, I guess I could of told you that, John.

JOHN: I wisht you woulda, Spider. It wouldn't of been any news to me, but I wisht you woulda. However, you had your reasons and no hard feelings. You'll be around next week as usual?

SPIDER: Sure. *I'm* with *you*, John.

JOHN: The way you say that, I better not count on Tony?

SPIDER: I aint gettin' any money from Tony. I'm gettin' my money from you.

JOHN: And supposing Ray Fallon made you an offer?

SPIDER: I aint as popular over at The Hall as some guys. They use me when they need me, if you know what I mean, but the rest of the time they like me to keep out of sight. The Hall is full of these guys that went to Fordham U, and I look too uncouth.

JOHN: You look all right to me, Spider boy. I didn't go to Fordham U either. I just took a course farther up the river.

Listen, I don't want you to say anything to Tony. Just tell him if he wants his money, he can come and get it. I'm entitled to the courtesy, the same courtesy you gave me, Spider.

Can I give you a ride uptown? I gotta get some clothes on.

SPIDER: Thanks a lot, John. I'm just going over't the poolroom.

JOHN: Keep one foot on the floor, boy. See you next week.

(*He puts a hand on* SPIDER's *shoulder and goes to the door with him. When the door is closed he makes a gesture of smacking his fist in the palm of his hand, at* SPIDER. *He goes to the phone, dials a number.*)

JOHN: Is this by any chawnce Miss Elizabeth Veronica Moore's residence? Miss Moore speaking? This is the Honorable Samuel Seabury speaking. Would you care to join me in a cup of tea and crumpets?

Huh? (*He smiles.*) You old bag, you get your ass over here. I wanta talk to you. Don't tell me over the phone. Tell me when you get here. Listen, I got somebody on the house phone. I gotta hang up.

(*He goes to the house phone.*)

Yeah?

Well, don't keep him waiting. Send him right up. . . . The *hell* with what I told you before.

(JOHN *is confused with excitement at the prospect of the next visitor. He looks at himself in the mirror, smooths down his hair, tries to make himself more presentable in his pajamas and dressing gown, lights a cigarette and puts it out as soon as the buzzer sounds. He goes to the door.*)

JOHN: Well, this is a pleasant surprise. Come right in.

(*A man of fifty or a little less enters. He is accustomed to respect. He is of Mediterranean origin, not readily identifiable by nationality. He wears a spotless pearl gray Homburg and an expensive double-breasted suit, a blue silk tie with a smoked pearl stickpin. He is a peasant and his clothes cannot hide that fact, but he has the manner of authority and strength and cunning.*)

JOHN: You by yourself? Let me take your hat, Mr. Benjamin.

MR. BENJAMIN: Downstairs in my car. I got a couple friends waiting. Where do you want me to sit?

JOHN: You're my guest. Anywhere it's comfortable.

MR. BENJAMIN: I like a straight chair. I got trouble with my back. Anybody else here?

JOHN: No, nobody.

Far From Heaven

MR. BENJAMIN: Spider Ray, the welterweight. He live in this building, or he come to see you?

JOHN: Oh, you saw the Spider. Spider Rattigan. Yeah, he was in to see me.

MR. BENJAMIN (*taking a chair*): One of your boys?

JOHN: Yeah. Old friend of mine. I give him fifty bucks a week.

MR. BENJAMIN: What for?

JOHN: Nothing, right now. But I may want to use him.

MR. BENJAMIN: For what? He isn't your bodyguard.

JOHN: No, I never had a bodyguard. I got him and another fellow to sort of run errands for me. I'm firing the other guy.

MR. BENJAMIN: Maybe you'll have to fire Spider Ray, too.

JOHN: Well, that wouldn't be any problem.

MR. BENJAMIN: Who did you like in the fifth race at Belmont?

JOHN: The California horse. Winaway.

MR. BENJAMIN: He has to beat the Whitney horse. I didn't bet that race. There was too many things to consider. I don't like to bet on a race with a big favorite like the Whitney horse and then a horse like this Winaway. Which is the other horse to beat but you'll see he goes off at ten-to-one. Maybe nine-to-one, but most likely ten-to-one.
What do you pay for this place, may I ask?

JOHN: Two-fifty. With maid service. Furnished.

MR. BENJAMIN: And you got the Polish girl living here now. Could I have a glass of water, please? No ice. Just a glass of plain water to sip. My throat gets dry. I played cards till seven o'clock this morning.

JOHN (*handing him glass of water*): How did you do?

TWO BY O'HARA

MR. BENJAMIN: I win a little. Stud I don't often lose at. Sociable game. Just some fellows. The big game I guess they're still playing. One o'clock this afternoon they were still playing. Charley B was way out in front then, but he's very erratic. By this time he could be playing with markers. Very erratic card-player, Charley B, but smart. He'll drop a big pot on a bluff, and the next time you figure him for a bluff, he has the cards. He sets you up for the phony bluff, you know what I mean.

JOHN: I never played in those big games.

MR. BENJAMIN: Oh, I know that. Pardon me for saying it, but where would you get the bankroll?

JOHN (*not angered*): I don't know, unless I stuck up a payroll.

MR. BENJAMIN: Most of the payroll stickups I hear about, they wouldn't consider that a bankroll in the game I was speaking of. Two thousand. Six thousand. Eleven thousand. They wouldn't let you play. They wouldn't even tell you where the game was. That kind of money, Mr. Sullivan, maybe they'd let you have a few rolls in the big dice game, but they don't want you in the big card game with a five-thousand-dollar bankroll.

What's the most money you ever dropped in a card game?

JOHN: In a card game? Oh, I guess I went for a thousand dollars a couple times.

MR. BENJAMIN: What's the most you ever win in a dice game?

JOHN: Shooting crap? Let me think.

MR. BENJAMIN: Round numbers.

JOHN: Six thousand dollars?

MR. BENJAMIN: Don't ask me, I'm asking you.

JOHN: About six gees, at Saratoga a couple years ago.

MR. BENJAMIN: And that's the most money you ever had in your life?

Far From Heaven

JOHN: Well, I'll tell *you.* I wouldn't tell everybody.

MR. BENJAMIN: Yes, please. Tell me.

JOHN: The most money I ever had at one time was a hundred and twenty thousand dollars. That was everything. I remember thinking I could live at the rate of ten gees a month for a whole year. I had the money stashed away---

MR. BENJAMIN: Don't tell me where you had it stashed. That's the kind of information, if we ever have to find it out we can. I never knew anybody didn't end up giving us the information.

JOHN: Yeah, I guess you play pretty rough.

MR. BENJAMIN: Just a minute, please.

(*He gets up and inspects the apartment, then returns.*)

I didn't tell you I was coming, because---

JOHN: You wanted to surprise me. That's all right. There's nobody here, and as far as I know, the place aint bugged.

MR. BENJAMIN: I'll be careful what I say. You want to come to work for me, Mr. Sullivan?

JOHN: I do.

MR. BENJAMIN: I'll give you a thousand dollars a month and I promise you two years' work to start. Minimum. After that, maybe you want to get out, and maybe I don't want you around no more. Or maybe you start making a lot more.

JOHN: A thousand dollars a month? I make more than that now.

MR. BENJAMIN: You *did* when you were the leader in this district, but those days are gone forever.

JOHN: You're sure of that?

MR. BENJAMIN: I'm as sure of that, Mr. Sullivan, as deep down in your heart you are too. If you didn't know that, you wouldn't be worth a nickel to me.

TWO BY O'HARA

JOHN: That brings up the question, why am I worth anything to you?

MR. BENJAMIN: You ask yourself that question, Mr. Sullivan.

(*He rises and hands* JOHN *a card.*)

Think it over a day or two, and then phone me at that number. That phone I answer myself.

Much obliged for taking up your time.

JOHN: I'll see you to the door.

MR. BENJAMIN: Thank you.

(*He accepts his hat and leaves.* JOHN *stands Down Center, holding the card in his hand.*)

JOHN: Twenty-four thousand dollars. A lousy twenty-four gees, for what I know. Why you cheap bastard.

(*He considers.*)

Twenty-four thousand dollars for a man's life. *My* life!

(*For the first time he knows fear. He shakes it off, but it comes back.*)

JOHN (*aloud*): You want to buy what I know for $24,000!

You want to give me a thousand a month for two years. You know God damn well I wouldn't be alive two years.

(*He tears the card in half, and then in instant terror, picks the torn halves off the floor. He sits on the floor, as though contemplating his fate, thinking. He gets laboriously to his feet and in a continuing action goes out of the room and returns immediately with a sponge-bag toilet kit. He turns it inside out and from inside the lining takes out several packages of new money. He puts the sponge-bag on the table and begins to count the money.*)

JOHN (*aloud*): One, two, three, four, five, six, seven, eight, nine, ten. One thousand. One, two, three, four, five, six, seven, eight, nine, ten. Two thousand. One, two, three, four, five, six (*he hesitates at the sound of the buzzer*), seven, eight, nine, ten. Three thousand.

(*He puts the counted money in one pile, away from the uncounted, and goes to house phone.*)

JOHN: Hello.

Who?

No. Tell her I---wait a minute. All right. She can come up. Son of a bitch, I forgot all about her.

(*He studies the piles of bills, decides he will not have the time to count them, and carefully replaces them in the secret lining of the sponge-bag, takes it back to the bathroom, and returns to the living room to await* PEGGY MOORE's *appearance.*)

JOHN (*aloud*): What the hell did I want with her?

(*He remembers, and when the buzzer sounds he opens the door.*)

JOHN: Bless my soul, it's Hedy. Come in, Hedy. Come wiss me to da Casbah.

PEGGY (*pretending to be annoyed, but liking it*): Aaaah.

JOHN: Take off your shoes. Loosen your girdle. And have a cigar.

PEGGY: Where is she? Out?

JOHN: Where is who? You referring to my secretary?

PEGGY: Yeah, your secretary. Alice. Alice in Wonderland. Where did you find her?

JOHN: You remember the song. The girl I love is on a magazine cover? She wasn't on the cover, but she was inside.

PEGGY: Inside the covers, huh? Under the covers. Wud you do, write her a fan letter?

TWO BY O'HARA

JOHN: No. But the day they sprung me, I went to the club where she was working, that same night. Got a knockdown, made the pitch, and she's with me ever since.

PEGGY: Well, one thing you did, John. You got hunk with Mona. You know I said to Mona, nearly two years ago, I said when John finds out about you and Ray Fallon, he's gonna start figuring how to get hunk with you.

"What can he do?" she said.

"I don't know what he can do," I said. "But he's figuring out something." You surprised me. I thought when you got out you'd come down and first beat the crap out of Ray, and then beat the crap out of Mona. But bringing a good-looking young broad like that around, that had the effect.

Gimme a snort, will you? Whiskey and water, half and half.

JOHN (*doing so*): Sure.

PEGGY: You surprised me. This way, when you wanta go back with Mona, you can. But if you'da thumped her around, I don't know. Mona wouldn't take a thumping, not even from you, John.

JOHN: *When* I wanta go back with Mona. That's a big when, like a big if. You saw what I got now. Why would I ever want to go back with Mona?

PEGGY: Well, I guess you probably must have laid fifty to a hundred broads at the same time you were laying Mona, but who'd you always go back to?

JOHN: Force of habit.

PEGGY: I aint saying it wasn't. But force of habit, that's as good as married life or falling in love with a person. It has the effect.

JOHN: Did you ever fall in love with a person?

PEGGY (*nodding*): Yes I did.

JOHN (*mildly surprised*): Who?

Far From Heaven

PEGGY: Why do you wanta know that? You don't think I was ever in love with a person?

JOHN: Well, you were kinda of busy there, Peg. You got started pretty early.

PEGGY: Yeah, I did. And I been a hustler since I was seventeen years of age. And you wouldn't touch me now with a ten-foot pole.

JOHN: If I had a ten-foot pole.

PEGGY: I know what you got, and what you aint got.

JOHN: Yeah. But that was when we were kids.

PEGGY: Well, when I was a kid was when I fell in love with a person.

JOHN: Who? One of our gang?

PEGGY (*slowly*): Yeah. . . . Willie.

JOHN: Willie Devlin?

PEGGY: Don't say it that way. It aint your place to high-hat Willie.

JOHN: Not high-hatting him, Peg. Just surprised.

PEGGY: Or surprised. Why should you be surprised? What did you ever know about Willie?

JOHN: To be honest with you, I never figured there was much to know.

PEGGY: No, you wouldn't. None of you did. He was the one that couldn't even finish the eighth grade. He was supposed to be a moron. *You* were the boy that got all the holy pictures and the rosary beads for being bright. But the only nice one in the whole damn bunch of you was Willie. The time the four of you got me up in James J. Callaghan's hayloft and put the blocks to me.

JOHN: Willie was in on that. He was one of the four.

TWO BY O'HARA

PEGGY: Yeah. But he came back and said he was sorry. He sat there with me till I stopped crying.

JOHN: Oh?

PEGGY: And walked home with me. *He* was *sorry*. Willie Devlin.

JOHN: I guess we all were, Peg. I got hell in confession. So did Stitch. So did What's His Name that moved away.

PEGGY: I don't mean that kind of sorry, John. I don't mean forcing yourself to be sorry so you can get absolution.

JOHN: I know.

PEGGY: No you don't. You don't have that in you, John. You're either born with it or you don't have it.

JOHN: So you fell in love with Willie. Then why didn't you wait and marry him?

PEGGY: Where's your memory? Your old lady and my old lady rushing the growler, or sitting in Dennie McDowd's every afternoon, swilling down the beer. I had to go to work just like anybody else, as soon as I was old enough to get a per*mit*. What for? So my old lady could swill down the beer with your old lady? I got wise to myself. And Willie? Was he any better off? The only time he could ever hold a job was if he shipped out. Deckhand. Cabin boy. Steward. And they wouldn't have him for a steward because he wasn't neat and tidy enough for them.

JOHN: . . . Me ask you something, Peg. Was Willie in love with you?

PEGGY: Well, he was never in love with anybody else. When he was on the beach I was his girl. His woman. He knew where the money come from, but he didn't taunt me with it. And when he couldn't stand it any longer around here, he'd ship out again.

JOHN: When did you quit being his girl?

PEGGY: Oh, it must have been around ten years ago. You remember when they threw him in the can? He stole some money?

Far From Heaven

JOHN: Sure. I went his bail.

PEGGY: That was the time. He was sent up for a little longer than you were.

JOHN: He done a little over two years.

PEGGY: Yeah. Well, when he got out I was working a hotel up on Forty-seventh Street and I didn't know he was out. So consequently I guess I didn't see him for over three years. We just got out of the habit, you talking about force of habit.

JOHN: But you still love him? Huh, Peg?

PEGGY: I just got finished telling you.
  You *heard* about Willie, I guess.

JOHN: If we're talking about the same thing, yes. Why?

PEGGY: That's why I wrote you the letter about Mona and Ray Fallon.

JOHN: Oh? Why?

PEGGY: Mona and her old lady kicked him out of the house. They coulda got him to go to the doctor, but instead of that they kicked him out. Well, that's why I wrote you the letter she was two-timing you. Who the hell is Mona? All the time she was laying you, you could of picked up a dose or big casino, and *she'da* had it. She had more chance of getting it from you than from her own brother. But it's too late for Willie now. Once it gets to your brain there's no cure for it, and he's been goofy a year, maybe more.
  Gimme another drink.

JOHN: Sure.

PEGGY (*while he refills glass*): The one I blame as much as I blame Mona is that Ray Fallon. I got no use for Mona. She was always a stuck-up kid, and when she got older she used to swing that ass of hers like she owned Twenty-third Street.

JOHN (*smiling*): You're right. You're right.

TWO BY O'HARA

PEGGY: But still and all, she got along all right with Willie. I think Ray Fallon put her up to it, kicking Willie out of the flat. I got no proof, but that's the way I figure it. Ray's in politics. He could of got Willie in some hospital. Maybe got him cured. But he wanted Willie out of there, out of the way. Just the same as he wanted you out of the way, John. You got a real enemy there. A slippery, conniving son of a bitch. I know people in this district that would just as soon cut your throat, if they could do it in the dark. A lot of people you done favors for had a good laugh when you got sent up. You were a good leader, John, but you rub some people the wrong way. You know it yourself, you do somebody a big favor and then you make some sarcastic remark for a joke, but they don't take it for a joke. So you got a lot of people here would like to spit in your eye. But you only got two real enemies.

JOHN: Ray Fallon, and who's the other? Tony Flanagan?

PEGGY: Well, maybe Tony Flanagan, but I wasn't thinking about him. In my book he's just a pinch of horse manure.
    No. You got Ray Fallon. And you got Edgar St. John.

JOHN: Edgar St. John? Why I put him in the same class that you put Tony Flanagan.

PEGGY: Have it your own way. But I know what I'm talking about.

JOHN: What's he got against me?

PEGGY: I don't know whether you do it on purpose, but every time he starts putting on airs, you slap him down.

JOHN: I do?

PEGGY: You never let him forget that his old man was a butler. A servant. I seen you do it fifty times.

JOHN: A butler? A butler aint just a stableboy, or a dishwasher. They make good money. My great-uncle was a butler in the Old Country and he ran the whole show. The stories I used to hear---

Far From Heaven

PEGGY: Edgar St. John's a geometry teacher, and the hell with what his old man was. You never hear him go around bragging about his old man being a butler. He wants everybody to think he's a highbrow professor. But you always get it in about his old man being a butler. A servant. You think the only way a man can show he hates you is if he takes a swing at you.

JOHN: No I don't think that. Give me credit for---

PEGGY: Then take a good look at Edgar the next time you mention butler.

JOHN: Matter of fact, Peg, Edgar St. John is a stooge and a stool pigeon. Anything I say he reports back to The Hall, and I found that out long ago. I didn't do anything about it, because I figured if that was the kind of a jerk they sent to spy on me, fine. If they could use him, so could I. Consequently, I feed him stuff that I know will get back to The Hall in an hour's time. Stool pigeon, yes. Stooge, I'll agree. But enemy---I don't classify him big enough to be an enemy.

PEGGY: Have it your own way.

JOHN (*good-humoredly*): Peg, I know this is an unusual request to make of you.

PEGGY: Yeah, what?

JOHN: Well, will you pardon me if I start putting my clothes *on*? I know it's usually the other way around with you.

PEGGY: As far as I'm concerned you can put them on or take them off. It won't bother me as long as you pour me another grog. . . . That dame coming back, or you going to meet her somewhere? I guess if you're putting your clothes on you going to meet her.

JOHN (*now starts going back and forth as he continues conversation while adding various garments*): The latter. I'm going uptown.

PEGGY (*goes to the window*): It started to rain out.

TWO BY O'HARA

JOHN: Is it raining hard?

PEGGY: Yeah, but I don't think it'll last.

(*Pulling on his pants he goes to the window and studies the rain.*)

JOHN: I don't know.

PEGGY: What don't you know?

JOHN: This rain. Which way's the wind blowing?

PEGGY: God, I don't know.

JOHN: This rain could cost me money. If they get a sloppy track out at Belmont, I got a horse that don't like the mud.

(*Goes to phone. Dials a number.*)

Hello, Johnny? Number 857. Yeah. Say, Johnny, it's raining down here where I am. What's it like out at Belmont?

Well what was the last report?

How long ago was that?

Yeah, but it just started here a couple minutes ago. This rain, you know, it could of come in from the Island. Or it could be from the west and going northeast. Five minutes of this and the track would be a mudpile.

Well, I'll call you later.

(*hangs up*)

They don't know nothin'. A half an hour ago it was a fast track, but a half an hour ago is ancient history by now. Say, look at it! When I was in the can I used to think to myself, I didn't care whether it rained or snowed or how hot or cold it got, I wanted to be outdoors the rest of my life. But I'm just as glad I'm inside now.

Hyuh, Peg?

(*He gives her a friendly tap on the behind.*)

PEGGY (*snorts, but not angrily at him*): Why?

Far From Heaven

JOHN: I don't know.

(*He is making an effort to be understanding, and she senses the fact.*)

PEGGY: Wudder you gonna do with yourself, John? They say you got paid off for going to jail, but what I heard, they don't want you back in politics. Is there any truth to that?

JOHN: Nothing but truth to it.

PEGGY: Then wudder you gonna do when you spent the payoff money?

JOHN (*cautious, if not quite suspicious*): You didn't happen to run into a visitor I had, just before you got here?

PEGGY: No. *Yeah.* There was a fellow waiting for the elevator when I got off. A kind of an Italian-looking, Greek-looking guy. Very stylish suit on, and a grey hat?

JOHN (*cagily*): Well you know who he was, don't you?

PEGGY: No. Should I of?

JOHN (*inventing*): Sure. Didn't you ever hear of Pasquale Volenti? One of the biggest spenders on Broadway.

PEGGY: Pasquale Volenti? I guess I heard of him. The name sounds familiar, but I can't place him. What does he do? What's he got going for him?

JOHN (*carried away with his own fiction*): Well, he's kind of an operator. He owns a big chain of dry cleaning stores out in the West. Pasquale Volenti.

PEGGY: Dry cleaning? You mean he's in some mob?

JOHN: Well---*he's* legitimate, as far as I know.

PEGGY: Did he own that big car that was standing downstairs? There were two guys sittin' in the back. John, you don't wanta get mixed up with the mob.

TWO BY O'HARA

JOHN: Pasquale Volenti, he's not a mob guy.

PEGGY: Those were hoods I seen in the back seat of that car. I know hoods when I see them. They took me for a fortune. Cops I don't mind paying. You pay a cop so you can stay in business, and he makes sure you *stay* in business. They give you real protection, the cops. But the mobsters, they take your money and all they do is ask for more. LaGuardia took the business away from the cops, and the hoodlums moved in. I hate every son of a bitch of a hoodlum there ever was. So don't get mixed up with *them*.

You want me to find out about this Pasquale Volenti?

JOHN (*cagily*): You saying you can get better information than I can?

PEGGY: Well, I guess not.

JOHN: Ask around, if you want to. Every little bit helps. Pasquale Volenti.

PEGGY: I'll remember the name.

JOHN: Owns a chain of dry cleaning stores out West.

PEGGY: Would that mean you had to move out of town somewhere?

JOHN: If I went in with him I probably would, yeah.

PEGGY: It'd be a great break for you. Not leaving New York, but there's nothing for you in politics here. And how many times does a guy get a good offer when he just got out of prison?

JOHN: That's what I *like* about Pasquale Volenti.

PEGGY: Just don't say yes till you're sure. Get all the angles.

JOHN: Right. That's why he wants me to come and work for him. A guy with my experience in politics, he figures me for a guy that looks at all the angles. I don't have to tell you, Peg. Be careful who you talk to.

PEGGY: Well, I won't talk to Ray Fallon, or Edgar St. John, if that's what you mean. Pasquale Volenti, from Chicago.

JOHN: No, I didn't say Chicago. That's not where he's from. Milwaukee, that's where he's out of.

PEGGY: Milwaukee. Well, they're all Chicago to me, out that way. Stopped raining.

JOHN: Stopped raining here. Belmont is where I want to know. You want another quick smash?

PEGGY: No thanks. I'll go now. . . . What did you want to see me about?

JOHN: Nothin'. I just wanted to have company.

PEGGY (*shaking her head*): You're taking it pretty good. I gotta give you that.

JOHN: How do you mean?

PEGGY (*rising*): The whole damn thing. You had a right to be good and sore, what they done to you, John J. Sullivan. When they took your picture down, that was the last straw.

JOHN (*hiding his surprise*): Yeah. Well, what's a picture if I'm not the leader no more? You know what LaGuardia's always saying. "A hollow mockery. A hollow mockery." Come around again, Peg.

PEGGY: Just give me a bell.

(*She leaves, and he stares straight ahead.*)

JOHN: Nobody. I got nobody. Not a son of a bitch in the world.

(*Wearily he dials a number, looking at his wristwatch, but with no animation.*)

JOHN: Johnny? This is 857.
I win? What'd he pay? Nine. Four. Two. I know, roughly. Nine hundred, four hundred, two hundred. How was the track?
Oh yeah? It musn't have rained at all out there.

No, I got nothin' more for today. Give you a call tomorrow.

(*hangs up*)

I should feel better than this. I don't feel a God damn thing.

(*He pours a drink, raises it, but halfway to his lips is as far as it gets. He makes a face at it and pours the whiskey back in the bottle. Curtain for End of Scene.*)

Act Two
SCENE
2

The apartment. Late at night. Several nights later. The living room is in darkness at Rise, which is immediately followed by the entrance, through the main door, of JOHN SULLIVAN *and* ALICE. *The door swings shut behind them and they switch on the lights. There are three men waiting for* JOHN, *and one of them goes to the door and stands with his back to it, with a hand in his pocket, obviously holding a gun.*

JOHN (*recovering from his surprise*): *Three* of you? What *is* it?

FIRST MAN: You'll find out.

(*to* ALICE)

You. You want to watch this, or you want to go in the other room?

JOHN: Now wait a minute, fellows. This---

(SECOND MAN *slaps his cheek and* JOHN *fights back but is expertly knocked to the floor.*)

Far From Heaven

JOHN: Let her go in the other room. Go on, Alice. You can't do anything.

(*Terrified but fascinated,* ALICE *leaves.*)

JOHN (*from the floor*): What's this for? Or do you know?

FIRST MAN (*to the other two*): Work on him.

JOHN (*getting quickly to his feet*): Wait a second.

(*He rushes the* THIRD MAN, *surprises him and gets in one good punch, knocking him over a chair.*)

JOHN (*laughing*): I took care of one of you, anyway.

(*But his sentence is not finished. He is struck by* SECOND MAN *with a blackjack, and goes down.* SECOND MAN *and* THIRD MAN *kick him all over the body and legs and on his arms, which are covering his head.*)

FIRST MAN (*who has remained at door*): Okay. That's it.

(*He goes to the bedroom door and calls to* ALICE.)

You in there. No cops, you hear?

SECOND MAN: He won't call the cops.

FIRST MAN: *He* won't, but maybe *she* might. Okay, let's go.

(SECOND MAN *takes a parting kick at* JOHN, *then the three of them leave. As the door closes, audibly,* ALICE *reappears. She kneels beside* JOHN.)

ALICE: You all right?

JOHN (*weakly*): I'm fine. Fine. Good exercise.

ALICE: You want me to call the doctor?

JOHN: Maybe. Not yet. I don't know.

(*With a little help from her he gets up off the floor and tumbles onto the sofa.*)

TWO BY O'HARA

ALICE: Who were they? What was that for?

JOHN: I don't know.
  We'll soon find out.

ALICE: How? The cops?

JOHN (*shakes his head and points to the phone*): No.
  Somebody'll phone. Ten. Fifteen minutes.
  My head. One of them sapped me. I got in one punch. Sapped me
from behind. Gimme a brandy, huh?

ALICE (*getting a brandy*): They coulda murdered you.

JOHN: Yep.
  But they didn't.
  Three of them, but they didn't kill me.

                (*takes brandy*)

  Didn't even kick me in the face. You notice that?
  A warning. Some kind of warning.
  I gotta puke.

ALICE: I'll get you something.

JOHN: No. Just help me up.

  (*She does and he goes off to bathroom, returning with a
  wet hand towel partially hiding his face. He sits down on
  the sofa again.*)

ALICE: Didn't you reccanize any of them?

JOHN: The Ritz brothers.

ALICE: No, seriously.

JOHN: Mannie, Moe and Jack.
  Faith, Hope and Charity.
  No. They were from Philly, or Bridgeport. One night's work.
Twenty-fi' dollars and expenses.

Far From Heaven

The guy at the door. You ever see him before?

ALICE: You think I fingered you?

JOHN: I don't think you fingered me. I just thought maybe you seen him before. I seen him before. But where, I don't know. He was the captain. The others, small-time hoods. The one that knocked me down, he coulda been a cop. An ex-cop. Jiu-jitsu. And he gave me the blackjack. Coulda been a small-town cop, up in the Catskills. What's the difference? I'll never find out. And what if I did?

ALICE: You gotta tell me what this is all about, John.

JOHN: Why?

ALICE: *Why?* The next time it may be me. I'm gonna send for my brother.

JOHN: You scared, Alice?

ALICE: You bet I'm scared. You were lucky. I saw some hoodlums work over a guy. Eeee-uhhh. That thing they do with a bottle, smashing the top of a bottle. Right down across his face. Ughhh. Makes me sick to think about it.

JOHN: I think they broke a rib.

ALICE: Who was it? Tell me.

JOHN (*As phone rings, he points to phone*): *Him.*

ALICE: Well, answer it.

JOHN: No.

ALICE: Annn-surrr ritttt! Find out what they want.

JOHN: Let them sweat.
    If I don't answer it they're gonna wonder why I don't answer it. Give the bastards something to worry about.

ALICE: You're crazy. They'll only beat you up again.

TWO BY O'HARA

JOHN: No.
 And keep your hands off that phone.

ALICE: It's driving me crazy.

JOHN (*Lifts phone from cradle, enough to break the connection when he hangs up again. The ringing stops*): Alice.

ALICE: What?

JOHN: Sure you weren't in on this?

ALICE: You're a stinkin' lousy bastard to ask me that. But I tell you something, you don't have to worry about me being in on the next one, because I won't *be* here. I'm getting out, John.

JOHN: You're taking a powder?

ALICE: You told me you hit one of them. What if he shot you? Then I'm mixed up in a murder. I thought you were a politician, but I think you're some kind of a mobster. The politicians *I* know, they don't even like you. Most of them don't even speak to you.

JOHN: Not any more, they don't. But as far as that goes, Alice, who does? Not so many speak to me any more.
 Oh, I'm sore. I hurt.
 All right, Alice. You can go. You want to go tonight?

ALICE: Well, God, I'll wait till tomorrow. I don't want to walk out and leave you by yourself. You may have internal injuries.

JOHN: I have internal injuries. I can feel them.

ALICE: I was talking about a hemorrhage.

JOHN: Oh, you want to take care of me? Be my night nurse? You're a good kid, Alice, and thanks. But if you think they're liable to come back tonight, maybe you better go. Because this time I'll be ready for them.
 (*With a great effort he gets up and goes to the escritoire, opens a drawer and takes out a .38 revolver.*)

JOHN: I never fired one of these. A belly gun, they call them.

ALICE: How did you know that?

JOHN: You seem to know it, too.

ALICE: My dead brother carried one.

JOHN: I wish he was here tonight. I'd sleep better. No, I don't mean that. They aint coming back. The only bother is gonna be from that (*pointing to the phone*).

ALICE: Put the gun away. You shouldn't have a gun around if you don't know how to use it.

JOHN: Don't tell me *you* know how to use it?

ALICE: No. But I'm glad I didn't know you had this one. I wouldn't of slept nights.

JOHN: I don't feel so good. I feel like I was dropped from a ten-story building.
   Alice, are you gonna be all right?

ALICE: How do you mean?

JOHN: You didn't stop to think of this, but you *saw* those three hoods. They're gonna remember that. I don't want to scare you, but maybe you better get lost.

ALICE: How do you mean?

JOHN: What they call go into seclusion. Detroit, or if your brother's in Cleveland. I don't care. I don't even want to know where you went. But right now those muzzlers are wishing you never got a look at their kissers. They should of jumped me as soon as I opened the door, but I turned on the light too fast.

ALICE (*meditating*): Mm-hmm.
   I don't have any money---or maybe seventy or eighty dollars.

JOHN: I'll let you have five hundred.

TWO BY O'HARA

ALICE: Five *hundred*? John, that isn't very much. How long will five hundred dollars last me?

JOHN: All right, I'll double it. I'll give you a gee. But I'm starting to run short.

ALICE: It isn't as if you gave me any jewelry, either. You know, I could of romanced you for a diamond bracelet.

JOHN (*doubtfully*): You think you could of? Maybe, but it's too late now, and a thousand dollars is the most I can spare. You better settle for that while I still got it.

ALICE: John, who sent those hoods?

JOHN: I honestly don't know. I could make a couple good guesses, but I don't want to accuse the wrong party.

(*The phone rings.*)

There he is again.

(*He lets it ring three times, then repeats the business of lifting and replacing the instrument.*)

JOHN: Now he don't know what to think.
And the worst of it is, he's itching to threaten me and I won't let him. He don't know *what* to think. He's thinking, am I alive or dead? Maybe one of his hoods kicked me too hard.

ALICE: Don't you have any curiosity what he wants to say?

JOHN: Plenty. But I'll hear soon enough. Right now I'm kind of needling him. Do you have some place you can go tonight?

ALICE: I guess so. She lives up on Central Park West.

JOHN: Who do you mean by she?

ALICE: I thought you didn't want to know.

JOHN: You're right I don't. But some girl friend?

ALICE: She always turns to me, and I always turn to her. She's out of show business now. Another one of us Polack girls.

JOHN: Don't tell me too much. . . . I want to wash my face.

(*He goes to bathroom, returning with a sheaf of banknotes in his hand.*)

JOHN: There's ten one-hundred-dollar bills, and here's two five-dollar bills. You want a fin to give the hack driver. You better start packing your clothes.

(*He goes to house phone.*)

Tommy? Sorry if I woke you up. Listen, Tommy, is there a hack downstairs? One of the regulars?

Well, tell him he got a job. My friend wants a ride uptown. She'll be down in a little while. Tell Louis it's a fi-dollar haul, that'll wake him up. Thanks, Tommy.

ALICE: You *want* me to leave.

JOHN: You'll be better off.

ALICE: You think they're coming back?

JOHN: No.

ALICE: I can't take all my clothes tonight. My trunk is in the basement.

JOHN: Take what you want. I'll put the rest in the trunk and leave instructions you'll call for it.

ALICE: I just as soon stay a while, John.

JOHN: Don't temp' me. I need sleep, Alice.

ALICE: I kind of feel like a rat, going now.
Is this the grand finale?

JOHN: Looks that way.

ALICE: You always treated me right, John. Except those times you kept me waiting.

TWO BY O'HARA

JOHN: As long as you don't have any regrets, Alice.

(*They move into an embrace, but he winces and cries out in pain.*)

JOHN: Ooh, Jesus.
You can see there's no use staying tonight.

ALICE: If I don't get married to somebody, I'll be back.

JOHN: Find yourself a nice big Polish boy. A tackle from Notre Dame.

ALICE: It won't be a Polish boy. They want to be the first.

JOHN: Well, find somebody.

ALICE: It's easy to find them. But holding on to them---

(*She goes to bedroom to pack, and while she is there the phone rings again.* JOHN *looks at it with loathing that is mixed with contempt. He thumbs his nose at the phone, then wearily sits down again. He lights a cigarette, but it makes him cough and he crushes it out. Then he repeats the phone-disconnecting business and the ringing stops. Then, on a sudden inspiration, he gets his wallet and takes out the card that had been given him by* MR. BENJAMIN. *He dials the number, listens for the signal, waits for an answer, then gently hangs up.*)

JOHN (*aloud*): That'll really screw you up.

(*Unknown to him,* ALICE *witnesses the business of dialing the phone. Then he turns and sees her, with her small suitcase in her hand.*)

ALICE: I don't get it.

JOHN: No, I guess you don't.

ALICE: But you *know* who sent those men.

Far From Heaven

JOHN: I told you, I can guess. Now I don't have to guess. I'm pretty sure.

ALICE: So long, John. Maybe I'll be seeing you, maybe not.

JOHN: Take care yourself, Alice.

(*With suitcase in hand she bends down and kisses him, then looks at him, just in case it is to be for the last time.*)

JOHN: What?

ALICE: I don't know. My mind is full of a lot of thoughts.

JOHN: You got everything you want?

ALICE (*laughing bitterly*): Huh. Jesus.

(*She extends a hand as though to pat his head, misses him, and in a continuing action goes out, letting the door swing shut behind her. Before he has any chance to soliloquize or think many thoughts about ALICE, the phone rings again. He repeats the disconnecting business, waits a second or two, then dials the number on BENJAMIN's card.*)

JOHN: Hello, Mr. Benjamin.
You know who this is.
Mr. Benjamin, I decided I didn't want to work for you. I don't like the way you treat your would-be employees.
I know I kept you waiting, but that's my privilege, aint it?
I got only one more thing to say to you, Mr. Benjamin. *I* got friends in town. Plenty of friends. Right here in town.

(*He hangs up gently, then*):

JOHN (*aloud*): Sure. Name one.

(*Curtain falls for End of Scene.*)

TWO BY O'HARA

Act Two
SCENE
3

The apartment. A week or so later. JOHN, *needing a shave, is wearing pajamas and slippers, without his dressing gown. On the table, an aluminum coffeepot and a paper container of cream, a cup and saucer. He has the* Daily Mirror *in front of him, and he is making up a list of horses to bet on. He sips the coffee, takes a drag on a cigarette. All but the smallest restricted movements give him pain, but he has grown semi-accustomed to it, so that while he winces, the pain does not interfere with his necessary activity. He picks up the phone, dials a number.*

JOHN: Johnny? This is 857. I got a lot of business for you.
Okay.

(He has been told to wait a minute.)

Hello, Johnny? Oh, *Harry.* Hello, Harry, what's with you, boy?
No, I been right here, but I been under the weather. A little touch of pneumonia, I think it was. I just been taking it easy.
Well, now I know *that,* Harry. I can tell you the exact amount. Right now it's a little over two gees.
Well, all right, so it's twenty-eight hundred? What's twenty-eight hundred with an account like mine? And listen, it'll be a lot less by nightfall. Comes the darkness, boy, and *you'll* be owing *me* money. In the second race at Baltimore, I like Greyboy. A hundred dollars on the nose.
No, I *won't* send you any cash.
No, *don't* send anybody down here for it.
Listen, how many years I been giving you all my bets?
Now wait a minute, fellow. Think back. What's the most I ever owed you?
Right. It was *over* six thousand, if you want to refresh your

Far From Heaven

memory. And was I good for it? You're friggin' well right I was good for it.

No, not half of it. No part of it. If you don't want to carry me now, say so, come out and say it like a man, but don't give me that malarkey about a thousand dollars on account.

All right, Harry. That's entirely up to you. But Harry? This is no time for guys in your racket to go around antagonizing. The Little Flower is making it very tough for you guys.

(*He looks at the mouthpiece;* HARRY *has hung up on him. He takes the rebuff more calmly than he would have in the past. He painfully gets to his feet and speaks into the house phone.*)

JOHN: Tommy? John Sullivan in 12-A.

Yeah. I wanted to get a couple bets down. What's the name of that guy runs the cigar store over on Eleventh Avenue, used to take bets?

Oh, he was, eh? Well, who would you suggest?

Uh-huh. If I called him up and told him who I was would he take a few bets for me?

Well, what if I mentioned *your* name?

No, I don't want to go over there myself. I gotta stay here all afternoon.

No. Thanks, Tommy. I just wanted to open an account with the guy. Forget it. I'll talk to you some other time.

(*hangs up*)

And you, Tommy Scanlon, that I got you your job. You won't let me use your name with a lousy two-dollar bookmaker. So you been hearing things, too, Mr. Tommy Scanlon. Well, you---

(*He is startled into silence as the house phone rings. He picks up the receiver.*)

JOHN: Yeah, Tommy?

Oh, all right. Send him up.

TWO BY O'HARA

On his *way* up? Listen, Tommy . . . (*but* TOMMY *has hung up on him. He hangs up.*)

(*The doorbell rings,* JOHN *opens it.*)

JOHN (*coldly*): Hello, Spider.
  I didn't see you for a while. You're getting like Tony Flanagan.

SPIDER: I missed a couple weeks because I hadda go out of town.

JOHN: Well, you take care of everything out of town?

SPIDER: Yeah. Yeah, I had a contract. I hear you been sick.

JOHN: Where'd you hear that?

SPIDER: Oh, a couple people.
  You broke up with the broad, huh?

JOHN: She returned to the convent.

SPIDER (*pompously*): Bad luck, making fun of religion.

JOHN: Get wise to yourself, you phony hypocrite. Wuddia want?

SPIDER: What do I *want*? I want three weeks' pay, a hundred and fifty bucks.

JOHN: Oh, you come to collect your pay. Oh.

SPIDER: The contract was fifty dollars a week, and it wouldn't interfere with my other contracts.

JOHN: Well, I tell you. While you were out of town I changed my mind. I made some alterations in the contract. Whereas party of the first part agrees to pay party of the second part, and so forth? I changed that, Spider. In other words, and plain language, balls.

SPIDER (*angered into silence*): Yeah?

JOHN: Not nuts. Not fiddlesticks. But balls, Spider.
  Was it a big contract out of town?

SPIDER: What's it to you, if it was big or little?

Far From Heaven

JOHN: What do you get for breaking a man's leg these days?

SPIDER: That depends on who the man is. A small-timer, you don't get a very good price. A big shot, you can collect. A politician that's all washed up, I might work him over for the fun of it.

(JOHN *slaps his face both ways, back and forth, and roughs him up generally, then* SPIDER *pulls away, retreating while he takes a switchblade from a pants pocket.*)

SPIDER (*knife in hand*): All right. Come at me again.

(JOHN, *keeping an eye on him, moves to the escritoire, reaches in the drawer and takes out the .38.*)

JOHN: It's a standoff, Spider.

SPIDER: No it aint. You hit me. You're ahead. But not for long, jailbird. You aint ahead for very long. Some people got *plans* for *you*.

(*He goes out.*)

JOHN (*in good humor*): Free information. The first time I don't pay him, he gives it to me for free.

(*He looks at the gun in his hand. He knows enough about it so that he can flip the chamber open and flip it shut. He holds it up and aims it at a picture on the wall, but then shrugs his shoulders and puts it back in the drawer.*)

JOHN (*aloud*): Plans for me? Well, now, who would know about that?

Mr. Ray Fallon. I can't call him. Miss Mona Devlin. Maybe. But I can't call her. Edgar St. John. Would he know? No. Spider knows a little, but not much. But if Spider knows a little, there's somebody that he talks to. And who is that somebody? As if I didn't know?

(*He dials a number.*)

Hello, Peggy? How're you, Peg?
John Sullivan? Didn't you reccanize the voice?

TWO BY O'HARA

Wuddia doing?

How about coming over and having a grog with me? I feel like
beating my gums.

Then how about later?

You're awful busy, Peg. You sure this isn't a tiny bit of the
brusheroo? You wouldn't be brushing me off, Peg. Not *you*.

Well how about if I paid you for your time? What do you get
these days, for a quick one? I remember when it used to be a half a
dollar, in the alley back of Dennie McDowd's.

Yes, I have a half a dollar, Peg.

Hold on to it? *Why* do you think I'm gonna need it, sweetheart?

Yeah, but that's only what you heard. I don't consider that
reliable information, what *you* heard. Who's gonna tell you
anything?

You want to know what I think, Peg? I think you're repeating
gossip, and that's a sin, you know. You're gonna have to tell that in
confession, repeating gossip. That's a sin on your immortal soul,
and if you die you're not gonna go straight to Heaven. Maybe you
won't even make Purgatory. You might get sent to the bad place.
H, e, l, l. Where the wicked are condemned. So you oughta be more
careful, repeating gossip like that.

Well, you take a good one for yourself, Peg. You need one worse
than I do.

(He hangs up.)

Well, that's a new low. The brushoff from the worst hooker in
Chelsea. Sullivan, you're getting nowhere fast. And now what? If
you had any brains, you'd blow them out.

(Begins to sing):

Mother dear, remember me!
Whilst far from heaven and thee—
I wander in a fragile bark
O'er life's tem-pes-tu-ous sea,—
O Virgin Mo-huther, from thy throne,

Far From Heaven

So bright in bliss abo-hove,—
Protect thy child and steer clear my path—*

My old lady! See what she has to offer.

(He dials.)

Hello, Mom?
It's Johnny.
Your son, for Christ's sake.
Yeah, he met me the day I got out.
You got the money, huh?
No, there won't *be* any more for a while.
Because I aint got any, that's why. You went through it awful
fast.
Joe has a job. He makes 300 a month.
Well, it looks like he's gonna have to support you too.
Listen, you got the seventy-eight a month from the old man's
pension. Make Joe give you twenty-two a month and you got an
even hundred. That'd be plenty, if you'd economize. Like drinking
a cheaper brand of whiskey.
To tell you the truth, I don't know why I called you. Yes I do, I
was just singing a hymn.
No, I'm not loaded. Mom, I gotta say goodbye. I'll see you when I
see you.

(He hangs up and reprises the hymn):

Mother dear, remember me!
Whilst far from heaven and thee—
I wander in a fragile bark
O'er life's tem-pes-tu-ous sea. . . .

(aloud)

When in doubt, consult with the enemy.

*The first line of this hymn is usually given as "Mother dear, O pray
for me!"

TWO BY O'HARA

(He dials.)

Hello, may I speak to Professor St. John?
He's still in class? Oh, no don't trouble him, Father.
Brother Casimir: Thank you, Brother Casimir. This is Father McDermott. No, not that Father McDermott. Another one. No, I'm not a Jesuit, Brother Casimir. Just a humble, ordinary parish priest. Professor St. John and I were boys together, a good many years ago, I'm afraid. I wanted to be a teacher, and he wanted to be a priest, but isn't that life? Things so seldom turn out the way we expect, Brother Casimir. Except through the power of prayer. Yes.

Well, I don't want to keep you away from your work. Would you take a message for my old friend? Would you ask him to call me at Chelsea 2-5566? That's correct, Brother. Chelsea 2-5566. I'm so anxious to talk to my dear old friend.

Thank you so much, Brother Casimir. God bless you.

(Daintily he replaces the phone.)

God bless you, you sweet old thing, Brother Caz. God bless you, too, my dear old boyhood friend. God bless everybody.

(He turns at sound of doorbell. Gets up to open it.)

And God bless you, whoever you are.

(He opens the door, and his whimsical mood vanishes.)

Oh. Hello, Mona.

MONA: Can I come in?

JOHN: Of course.

(He stands aside to let her in, then goes to bedroom and returns putting on dressing gown. She looks at the coffee-pot, etc., quickly sizing up his situation, and obviously confirming what she has heard.)

JOHN: You want a cigarette? How about a drink? I could heat you some coffee. Or I'll make some fresh.

MONA (*shaking her head, lighting her own cigarette*): I didn't know Tommy Scanlon worked here.

JOHN: Yeah, I got him the job, just before I went on my vacation up the river.

MONA: Then he's a friend of yours?

JOHN: No, I don't say that about anybody these days. It's liable to get them in trouble with that, what's his name, Ray Fallon. No, Tommy Scanlon's no friend of mine. Why?

(*The hostility he shows her is pretty well controlled; if he did not permit himself this show of hostility he would have to reveal the deeper emotion, the intense hatred of her. The hostility is a kind of safety valve.*)

MONA: He used to be a big mouth. He could never keep anything to himself.

JOHN: Meaning, I suppose, that Mr. Ray Fallon didn't send you here?

MONA: I came of my own accord.

JOHN: Why?

MONA (*not answering him*): If Ray knew I was here that'd be the end of him and me. Why did you have to tell him about Asbury Park? Why did you have to say we were together a thousand times?

JOHN: Oh, I just wanted him to know he had a long way to go before he knew you as well as I did.

You were gonna wait for me till I did my time. You waited about two weeks, not two years. You made a real monkey out of me, you *and* Fallon.

It was gonna be so easy up there. I'd get a soft job in the prison library. Special privileges. A lot of visitors. I wasn't a guy that shot somebody or done any of those things. I was a kind of a political prisoner. Bert Ryan. Bert Ryan and your friend Mr. Ray Fallon,

they as much as promised me I could be alone with a woman once a
month, meaning you.

But I soon found out.

They treated me just like anybody else. I said to the guard one
day, I said when do I start working in the library? He laughed at
me. He said I ought to be able to do two years standing on one foot.
I never got any special privileges. I got some taken away, a couple
times.

I was there about three weeks and I got a letter about you and
Fallon.

(*He pauses to relive those moments.*)

You and Fallon.

I did seventeen more months, thinking about you and Fallon.
Seventeen months I talked to myself. The other cons said I couldn't
take it. I was stir crazy when I was only there a month. I still talk to
myself, so maybe they were right.

Now do you know why I told Fallon to ask you about Asbury
Park?

MONA: He asked me, all right.

JOHN: Well, I hope you told him.

MONA: I told him.

JOHN: Well, he had you for seventeen months anyway.

MONA: That was different. Everybody knew I was your girl, but all
you had to do was mention one place, and that changed everything
for Ray. He had to know about Asbury Park and every place else.
Ever since you said that, everything reminds him of you.

JOHN (*lights a cigarette and takes a long drag*): I wasn't the only
guy you ever went to bed with.

MONA: He knows that.

JOHN: Well, wuddia want me to do, Mona? Go and tell him

Far From Heaven

nothing ever happened? We had one of them Platonic friendships? We rubbed noses? In other words, what the hell did you come here for?

MONA: Who is a man named Benjamin? I don't know whether it's his first name or last name.

JOHN (*fishing*): I know a lot of Benjamins. First name *and* last name.

MONA: This one you're better acquainted with.

JOHN: You'll have to describe him for me.

MONA: I only saw him the one time, but he's dark complected. Around your age or a little older. Expensive clothes. Uses fingernail polish. Puts cologne on his handkerchiefs. Are you trying to find out how much I know about him? Well, not much. But he's with Ray. He's with him now. Ray, Bert Ryan, Goldberg, and Edgar St. John.

JOHN: Maybe they're getting ready to give me a welcome-home party.

MONA (*humorless*): If they invite you to anything, don't go to it.

JOHN: All right, what is it?

MONA: I'm living with Ray. You knew that, I guess.

JOHN: Go on.

MONA: A couple nights ago I was asleep in bed. Ray wasn't home yet. Then he came home and he had two men with him. He looked to see if I was asleep, then he shut the door and they began talking, the three of them. I didn't pay any attention till I heard them mention your name.

   Did you go to Benjamin and offer to sell out? Tell him everything you know?

JOHN: No.

TWO BY O'HARA

MONA: He said you did. And they believe him. Bert Ryan believes him, and Ray believes him.

Listen, John. I wouldn't be telling you this except for one thing. Bert Ryan, and Ray, they both believe Benjamin because you're supposed to be sore on account of me. Ray and me.

JOHN: Well-well.

MONA: Bert Ryan is convinced of it. You got rid of the Polish girl because you were in love with me.

JOHN: That's so romantic for Bert.

MONA: You hate Ray so much that you went to this Benjamin and offered to sell out, everything you know.

JOHN: Why would Benjamin be so interested?

MONA: Why wouldn't he be? A racket guy that knew all you knew---

JOHN: What racket?

MONA: You tell me. But that's what Benjamin is, and if you spilled everything you knew, Benjamin would have a lot of information. He'd be sitting pretty with the men over at The Hall.

JOHN: An excellent analysis. Did you figure it all out yourself?

MONA: No. Bert Ryan did. Benjamin went home, but Bert and Ray stayed up talking for a couple hours. Bert is real worried.

JOHN: Bert's a worrier.

MONA: He doesn't want to have to do business with Benjamin, but now he has no choice in the matter.

JOHN: So it would seem.

MONA: What kind of a dirty racket is it Benjamin's in, that Bert's so squeamish?

JOHN: There's no racket too dirty for Bert. He just doesn't want to do business with Benjamin. Bookmaking. The numbers. Girls.

Far From Heaven

Dope. Unions. Bert owns a cemetery. A limestone and gravel business. A fleet of cabs. Mind you, he don't own them all personally, but they're all legitimate fronts. You be surprised how many little Jewish stationery-storekeepers own a plot in Bert's cemetery. Those are the two-dollar bookmakers. They're all gonna turn Catholic before they die, or why else would they buy a plot from Bert? Bert's in everything where there's a dollar, and once you let a smart fellow like Benjamin get his foot in the door---that's all he needs.

I'm a very small guy, compared to what there is. I never got higher than leader. I ate good, liked the booze, always had a few dollars going for me at the track. I wore silk underwear, you may recall, and if it wasn't you, it was some other female companion. My big trouble was I had no ambition. You look at Bert, or for that matter, that dreary son of a bitch you're tied up with---serious, no laughs. Bert Ryan looks like he started every day with a pickle for breakfast. And your guy, Mr. Fallon, he's afraid of his own shadow. He'd like to be me, but he don't know how. So, maybe he'll end up on the National Committee. Do you love him?

MONA: I don't love anybody.

JOHN: I don't think you *do*. That's what two years with Mr. Fallon did for you. When you were with me nobody had to ask you that question. You stuck out your chest and you swung your tail, and anybody could see you were getting what you wanted with the guy you wanted it from.

And I'll be a son of a bitch, the same thing held good for me. *I* felt good. I didn't want to get elected to Congress, I didn't want to be County Chairman. Settle down and run for Congress, they used to tell me. Get to be County Chairman. What the hell for?

But then your Mr. Fallon---

MONA: Oh, shut up about Mr. Fallon.

JOHN: *You* shut up. I got things stored up inside of me. Your Mr. Fallon thought he'd like to have a little piece of you, and a little job up in Albany. He wanted to be me, God damn it.

TWO BY O'HARA

Well, he aint. He double-crossed me with Ryan, and he went after you and you were a pushover for him. But he aint me.

Why'd you come here, Mona? Are they gonna knock me off? You wanted to warn me? Does Bert Ryan think I'm so unimportant that I won't be missed?

MONA: You better listen to me a minute.

JOHN: Why? I know why you're here. Well let me show you something.

(*He tears off his upper garments to show his beaten torso.*)

I took one beating.

MONA (*horrified*): Who did that?

JOHN: Some friends of Mr. Benjamin, because I *wouldn't* sell out. But the next time it won't be Mr. Benjamin's boys. And they won't just give me the boot. It'll be your boys, Mona. And I been sitting here waiting for them. With this.

(*goes to escritoire and takes out .38*)

MONA: John!

JOHN: Yeah. It's gonna be pretty noisy around here for a couple minutes. I figure in about a week's time. They gotta get somebody from out of town, a gunsel, maybe two. But they can't put it off much longer. Bert thinks I'm ready to talk, I might even talk to Dewey. Seabury. LaGuardia. No, not Seabury. Rest assured I'll never talk to him. I wouldn't know how to say prostitute in front of him.

Do you want to know what I found out about Sam Seabury? When I was in prison I used to read books, and you know what? Old Seabury's great-great-grandfather didn't even like George Washington. That's an absolute fact.

I couldn't talk to *him*.

MONA: You better talk to somebody, for your own protection.

Far From Heaven

JOHN: That---from Ray Fallon's girl?

MONA: I'm not his girl. I'm his wife.

JOHN: The hell you are.

MONA: I been married to him over a year.

JOHN (*quickly*): What church?

MONA: No church. We got married upstate, Troy. Troy, New York. I was three months pregnant---

JOHN (*mental arithmetic*): Three months. Then it wasn't me.

MONA: No, it wasn't you. We got a judge to marry us and we didn't tell anybody. Then I lost the baby. But I'm his wife.

JOHN: And even more delightful, he's your husband. Well, this calls for some kind of a celebration. What would you like for a wedding present? I coulda knitted you something while I was in the can. A lot of cons take up knitting, a certain type of con. They do *beautiful* work.

MONA (*wearily*): Oh, Christ.
  You stupid son of a bitch, you're in trouble.

JOHN: Well, if you don't think *you're* in trouble---

MONA: Not your kind of trouble.

JOHN: This is the kind of information Tommy Scanlon would relish. He wouldn't go to your husband, Mr. Fallon. With this kind of information he goes direct to Bert Ryan. (*Imitating* TOMMY SCANLON): "Mr. Ryan, I wouldn't entrust this to nobody but you, but John Sullivan had a visitor, none other than Mona Devlin. And be the way, Mr. Ryan, would there be an opening for me brother if I sent for him. He can't find work in Ireland, and he's a sober, honest, reliable man." Tommy Scanlon's brother, if he has one, is as good as digging graves in Bert Ryan's cemetery this minute. And he'll never know who to thank.

TWO BY O'HARA

MONA: You don't want to listen to me.

JOHN: I *been* listening to you, Mona, and you didn't tell me anything I didn't know with the exception of your belated wedding announcement. If there's more, I'll be willing to listen, but. . . .

MONA: Are you just gonna sit here and wait?

JOHN: Till I'm dispossessed. I'm paid up till the first of the month, then they have to get an order to---

MONA (*partially ignoring him*): You're going to wait here till some night they come again and beat you up, if that's all they do. And you have a gun, so maybe you'll shoot one of them. Is that how you want to die, John? Kicked to death, or shot with a pistol?

JOHN: No. I always wanted to go out a big hero, but I wasn't cut out for that. I'm a kind of a slob. I done a lot of favors for people, but I never had no respect for anybody. John McGraw. I guess maybe I patterned myself after Muggsy, in some ways, although he wasn't much of a guy for laughs. Now all those people I made fools of, they're starting to laugh at me.

If I had any real sense, I should of stopped and thought a minute when I heard about you sleeping with Fallon. I should of asked myself, why did she get in the hay with that dreary bastard. Now I know why. You were the first one to get hunk with me, Mona. Nearly two years ago. All the time you and I were romancing, I'd lay some other dame and you'd get sore but you didn't stay sore. So I did the same thing over again. Only what I didn't realize, you did stay sore, and that's why as soon as I was out of the way, you took off your drawers for Mr. Fallon. What's he like, Mona? Did he find out what you like?

MONA: Respect. He found out I liked respect.

JOHN: But you don't. Don't kid yourself. You never wanted respect. You got what you wanted from me, which was a good lay, and then me going out and laying some other dame, and then you and me having a fight and a good lay to make up. For six years that's the way it was, and that's what you wanted. But I don't say that's all. It aint nearly as simple as that, Mona.

Six years, and then you wanted a change. So you took on Mr. Fallon, kidding yourself that you were getting even with me. But what you really wanted was another man.

MONA: I wanted someone that I could love, and that loved me.

JOHN: That's where you kid yourself. We had love, you and I. That was love. You said a while ago you don't love anybody. You were right. You don't. Neither do I. You want to know something? We had a perfect love. Absolutely perfect for you, and for me. But everybody's different. You and I were a couple of selfish bastards that loved all we can, and that ended it. You two-timed me with Fallon, and I changed into hating you. But the real fact of the matter, Mona, we just wore out as far as love is concerned. You going to bed with Fallon and me hating you for it---nothing. We just wore out. Everything wears out. Take me. A politician. Supposed to be a glad-hander. A backslapper. But I never was. I went around insulting people to their faces, and they loved it. You know why? Because I was a politician, and they didn't think a politician meant it when he made insulting remarks. But I did. I used people for laughs, and they went along with the laugh. Then I got thrown in the can, and they got used to this bastard Fallon, a dreary son of a bitch that'd be afraid to insult a voter. The people I used to insult began to get their self-respect back, and I was through. You can insult a guy if you see him every day and he depends on you for favors. But don't try it when you've been away for a while, and you can't do them any favors. Don't ever let a guy find out you're using him for laughs.

You came here to tell me they're probably gonna kill me. Maybe they are. If I was Bert Ryan in the same situation, I wouldn't know what else to do. I know too God damn much. First degree murder is a hell of a rap, but it's worth the risk. You can get away with first degree murder in this town. It's been done. Right in this district. No, I wasn't in on any of them, but if a guy gets suddenly dead, you usually know why. I went to prison because I wouldn't talk. They persuaded me to go, and they paid me. Well, they'd pay me in a different way if they figured I was going to talk after all. Everybody will know why I got knocked off, but try and prove who did it.

MONA: You're not that brave. Why don't you get away?

JOHN: To where? If you could guarantee me a place, I'd go there. The only chance I got is if I stay here and shoot it out.

MONA: You're out of your mind.

JOHN: Am I? I'd be out of my mind to run. If I went to some place like Indianapolis, Houston, Texas---I'd only make it easy for them. What the hell would the Indiana cops care if a New York politician gets knocked off by person or persons unknown?

But if I stay here I have this much of a chance. Maybe they won't kill me, maybe I'll get lucky and kill them. *And*, if they don't get me, it'll be Bert Ryan's turn to run, because then I really will talk.

MONA (*gets up and takes off her hat*): All right.

JOHN: Explain the business with the hat.

MONA: I'm staying.

(*She starts picking up the coffeepot and the dirty cups and saucers, etc. He frowns at her, but he fully understands that she is determined to stay, and slowly he smiles. Curtain for End of Scene and Act.*)

Act Three
SCENE
1

The apartment. Next day. MONA, *wearing bra, slip, and panties under* JOHN's *Sulka dressing gown, is busy getting breakfast. He, in pajamas, enters from bedroom. His hair is brushed but he still needs a shave. He goes to her, in the midst of her breakfast table setting, and wordlessly puts his arm around her waist. She turns around and embraces him with affection without passion. She is here to stay, they are reunited, and they need no words to express it. The very fact that the usually garrulous* JOHN *is silent is significant. They end the embrace, she resumes her work.*

MONA: I have to figure out some way to get my clothes.

JOHN (*from habit*): Buy some new ones.

MONA: We're gonna need every cent, and anyway I won't take anything he paid for.

JOHN: I just as soon you didn't go back to that apartment.

MONA: I'm not going back if I can help it. Do you want orange juice?

JOHN: Yeah, I'd like some orange juice. There's a bottle of it in the icebox. You don't have to squeeze it.

MONA: You want a big glass or a small one?

JOHN: Oh, big, I guess.
 I'm surprised we didn't have a phone call from Fallon.

MONA: Well, as soon as we have our breakfast *I'll* phone *him.*

TWO BY O'HARA

JOHN: Yeah, let's get that settled right away.

(*He gets the sponge-bag and opens it.*)

The Chase National Bank.

(*extracts a sheaf of bills*)

Two, three, four, five, six, six-fifty, seven, seven-fifty. That's the bankroll.

MONA: That's all you have left?

JOHN: That's it. I even owe that. I'm welshing on some bets or I wouldn't have this much.

MONA: The bookmaker? Harry?

JOHN: Yeah. I'm in him for twenty-eight hundred.

MONA: Well, he's way ahead.

JOHN: He sure is, but it goes against my grain, welshing. Mind you, he don't get a nickel of this. But all the same, I don't like to welsh.

MONA: Your juice. The coffee's almost ready. I don't see any butter for the toast.

JOHN: I guess I used it all up. There's some marmalade, though.

MONA: I see it. You ought to learn to put the top back on the jar. I got some money I can draw out of the bank. It's over fifteen hundred dollars.

JOHN: Seven-fifty and fifteen hundred. Twenty-two-fifty. We'll need it. I got my star sapphire. I won't get near what I paid for it, but it might bring four-five hundred. And my presentation watch, they presented me with. It's a Patteck-Phileep. That and the chain oughta be worth five bills. I lost my gold cigarette case but I still got the gold lighter you gave me. We can hold on to that stuff till we get to the coast, and maybe we won't have to hock it *if* I make a quick connection.

Far From Heaven

MONA: Your coffee. It's plenty strong.

JOHN: I still like it strong. Do you have any of the stuff I gave you?

MONA: The ring, and the bracelet. At the apartment.

JOHN: Then I guess you can kiss it goodbye.

It's gonna cost us to leave town.

They know I'm low in the dough, so they're gonna look for us at all the bus stations.

MONA: They can't have somebody at all the bus stations. There's too many of them.

JOHN: Mr. Bert Ryan can fix that. He can call the Police Commissioner and ask him as a favor, unofficially have the cops cover the bus stations. So what we do, it's gonna cost us, but we get reservations on the Century. After we get to Chicago we can travel by bus. Save money *that* way. And see more of the country. We can be in Los Angeles in about a week. We get off the bus at the last stop before Los Angeles, and take a local bus line from there on in. I wish I knew how to get in touch with Jimmy Cagney.

MONA: Do you know him?

JOHN: I think he'd remember me. Him and Pat O'Brien came to one of our benefits a couple years ago. Jimmy did a tap dance, and O'Brien's a very good storyteller. Well, we'll see when we get there.

You wanta look up the number of the New York Central for me?

(She gets the phone book.)

MONA: Sleeping car reservations. Murray Hill 7-6600.

JOHN: Me think up a good name. I wanta sound important, but not phony. Colonel. Colonel Something. Colonel and Mrs. Colonel and Mrs. J. J. Sully. That sounds like an army name, Sully. And the initials are the same.

(dials phone)

TWO BY O'HARA

Reservations? On the 20th Century Limited this afternoon, this is Colonel J. J. Sully. Could I have a drawing room for two this afternoon? Colonel J. J. Sully.

Well, I'm over on Governors Island and I may not be able to pick them up till quite late. Do I have to send my orderly? I promise you, I'll be there a half an hour before train time. That'll be two, for Mrs. Sully and myself. Colonel J. J. Sully. Right-ho, thank you very much.

(hangs up)

A Boy Scout. Very impressed by the "colonel."

I feel good. I feel like I'm doing something. This time yesterday I didn't give a good God damn.

(He reaches out and presses her hand.)

Now let's put the brain to work on getting you your clothes.

MONA: I have a key, if I can get somebody to go over there.

JOHN: First we want to make sure Fallon is out.

MONA: You bet.

JOHN: We have to find somebody you can trust. Who is that? I say nobody. But who don't you distrust more than the others?

You know who'd do it in a minute, believe it or not?

MONA: Who?

JOHN: Alice. The Polish kid I had here.

MONA: No.

JOHN: Well, she's out anyway, because I don't know where she is. But she'd do it.

MONA: I'm trying hard to think.

JOHN: Does it have to be a woman? You could make out a list, what you want and what closet it's in, and some guy could get it.

Far From Heaven

MONA: A suit and a dress, a couple pairs of shoes, and some underclothes.

JOHN: You start making out the list and where they all are.

(*She picks up a pencil, and smiles at him.*)

MONA: You know you're right? This time yesterday I didn't give a damn, either. Have some more coffee.

JOHN: Gimme your cup. You have some too.

MONA: Thanks.

JOHN: You want a cigarette?

MONA: Yeah, I guess so.

(*He is handing her a cigarette and the doorbell rings.*)

JOHN (*looks at the clock*): That's the cleaning woman. Tell her we don't need her. Come in tomorrow.

(MONA *goes to the door, opens it, and is pushed aside by* RAY FALLON.)

FALLON (*looking at* MONA, *then at* JOHN): I would of bet on it.

JOHN: You would have? Not me. I'd of *taken* your bet.

FALLON (*to* MONA): Get your clothes on. I'll talk to you later.

JOHN: I didn't hear you say good morning. You're the leader now, you're supposed to be polite to we voters.

FALLON (*trying to ignore him*): You heard what I said, put your dress on. I didn't come here to talk to this jailbird.

JOHN: Relax, Fallon, relax. You're acting like a jealous husband.

FALLON: I am her husband.

JOHN: You were, but I gave her a divorce. We annulled it (*laughs*). It was a secret marriage, so we performed a secret annulment.

TWO BY O'HARA

She's not going back with you, Fallon. We set up housekeeping, and Mona's staying here with me.

I'll level with you. By tomorrow we'll be in Florida, and the next day we'll be in Havana. And it's no use trying to stop us. I got friends in Miami that you never even heard of, but they're very hard boys. Very hard.

Now you go back to that judge up in Troy and see if he'll fix you up with a quiet divorce. Quiet wedding, quiet divorce. Forget all about Monar and I, and if you ever come to Havana---well, don't come too soon, but next year, the year after, when there's no hard feelings, we'll throw a party for you.

FALLON (*to* MONA): Do you go for this line of crap? I'll ask you once more, are you coming with me or aren't you?

MONA: No.

FALLON: You had your chance. Maybe he got you drunk or something, but if I go out that door without you, that's the last you'll ever see of me.

JOHN: I coulda told you, Fallon. She's as changeable as the weather. Do us a favor, will you? When you get the divorce, send us the papers care of the Hotel Nacional, Havana, Cuba.

FALLON: Mona.

MONA: What?

FALLON: I promise you, I won't hold it against you.

MONA: I'm not going with you, I'm staying with him.

JOHN: She may be changeable, Fallon, but she's not gonna change that quick. She only came back with me last night. The least you can give her is a little time.

FALLON: She don't have any time (*turns fully on* JOHN). And you, you son of a bitch, you don't either.

(*He storms out.* MONA *lights another cigarette.*)

Far From Heaven

MONA: He didn't swallow that about Havana.

JOHN: Don't bet me, Mona. I said it like I was bragging. If I said it any other way he wouldn't believe me, but the loudmouth braggart he'd believe. I wasn't trying to convince him. He'll convince himself.

MONA: Maybe. You probably know him better than I do. Just now it was like I never knew him at all.

JOHN (*his spirits expanding*): I told you, he wanted to be me. You had a guy trying to be me, but now you got the real thing.

Listen, kid, I got my confidence back. We got a couple tough weeks ahead. Maybe it'll take a month before I make the right kind of a connection out there. But I get out there and through Cagney or O'Brien or one of those movie guys, I get on my feet, and back here they're gonna stop worrying about me. You see how I got my confidence back? You did that for me. Honest. All I had to have was you, partnering up with me. No other son of a bitch in creation could do that for me, Mona. Only you.

MONA: Well, I wish we were there now.

JOHN: But I'm gonna keep you away from those Hollywood guys. Not Jimmy, or Pat. I was thinking more of those Hollywood wolves.

MONA: They wouldn't pay any attention to me.

JOHN: Oh, they wouldn't? What about me? I went for that young gash, too, but I always came back to you. And I always will, Mona, no matter what.

MONA (*tolerantly but lovingly*): I hope so.

JOHN: Yop. Colonel J. J. Sully is an officer and a gentleman.

MONA: Who is---oh.

(*She smiles and begins to remove the breakfast things as Curtain descends for End of Scene.*)

TWO BY O'HARA

Act Three
SCENE
2

Later the same day. JOHN *is fully dressed except for his suit coat. His large suitcase, packed and closed, is plainly visible.*

JOHN: You know, I been thinking, Mona. Why don't we wait till we get to Chicago tomorrow. You can buy a suit there.

MONA (*She also has a dress on, shoes, etc.*): I was thinking the same thing. But it isn't only my clothes I want. We may wish we had my diamond ring and my bracelet. They ought to bring a thousand dollars between them.

JOHN: I don't want you going to that apartment.

MONA: I could be there and back inside of ten minutes. I won't stop to get any clothes. I'll just get the ring and the bracelet. You know what'll happen if I don't get them?

JOHN: Fallon will keep them.

MONA (*shaking her head*): No. Nobody will keep them. Nobody'll ever see them again. I got them hidden, stuck inside of a jar of cold cream. Ray'll throw the cold cream away with the garbage and they won't be worth anything to anybody. A thousand dollars in the garbage can.

JOHN: A hell of a lot more than a thousand dollars they cost me. Well, if you want to take a chance. Call up and see if he answers.

(*She dials, shakes her head, hangs up.*)

MONA: He's very seldom there this time of day. I'll be back inside of ten minutes.

JOHN: Well, if you're not I'll come and get you.

(*Over-casually he goes to the escritoire and opens the drawer. She watches him intently, knowingly.*)

Far From Heaven

MONA (*She points to the suitcase*): That thing you're looking for. You packed it.

JOHN: So I did. I think I'll put it in my pocket.

MONA: I wish you'd throw it away.

JOHN: It may come in handy, and they're not so easy to get in a strange town.

MONA: All we need now is to have some cop arrest you on a phony charge, and they find a gun in your pocket.

JOHN (*seeing the wisdom of this*): You're right. But all the same I'm gonna take it along in the suitcase. . . . Well, if you're going, you better go. (*With a slight flourish he looks at his pocket watch and his wristwatch.*) If you're not back in---well, I'll give you fifteen minutes.

MONA: I'll be back in ten or less.

(*She kisses him and pats his cheek, and he smiles.*)

JOHN: I love you, God damn it.

(*She nods happily and exits. He stands, frowning at the suitcase, considering whether to remove the gun, then decides not to. At this the doorbell rings, and he goes to answer it.*)

JOHN (*belligerently*): Yeah. Wudda *you* want?

A SMALL MAN IN A DELIVERYMAN'S UNIFORM: Sullivan?

JOHN: Could be, could be.

DELIVERYMAN: I got a package here from Pastorius & Chilling-worth.

JOHN: Oh, my Tuxedo! Come in. You want me to sign for it?

DELIVERYMAN: Yes sir.

JOHN (*pleased and somewhat excited*): They finally got it finished, eh?

TWO BY O'HARA

DELIVERYMAN (*holding out a receipt book*): Yeah, I guess so. Will you sign your name down at the bottom there, where it says received by.

JOHN: I shall be pleased to affix my signature, my good man.

(*He does so, then from force of habit takes out a roll of bills and wets his thumb, but changes his mind and fishes out a 50-cent piece from another pocket.*)

DELIVERYMAN: Thanks.

JOHN: Go with God.

DELIVERYMAN: Wha'?

JOHN: So long, pal.

DELIVERYMAN: Oh.

(*He exits, annoyed and baffled, and* JOHN *immediately eagerly tears open the package. He takes out the Tuxedo and tries it on, looking at himself in a wall mirror, and then he bursts out laughing.*)

JOHN (*aloud*): Jesus Christ. The irony of it. The irony.

(*Nevertheless he takes out the pants and holds them up against his leg.*)

JOHN (*aloud*): A hundred and eighty-five bucks.
 Well, a hundred and eighty-five bucks I didn't pay, but what a pity. Looka the way that collar fits.

(*He studies himself in the mirror, admiring the sleeves, the roll of the lapels.*)

JOHN: I wonder if I got room for it.

(*begins to act out an imaginary scene*)

 Why if it isn't Jimmy Cagney. Why hello there, Jim boy. Say, there's Pat O'Brien. It looks like Irish Night in Beverly Hills.
 Oh, this? Pastorius & Chillingworth. I get all my clothes there.

They cost me, but I'm very hard to fit. Why there's Crosby over there. Excuse me while I go say hello to the Groaner.

Well, I don't know very much about picture business, but I might be willing to learn. If you made it worth my while, you fellows. We politicians, one thing you gotta say for us. We know what the public wants. Okay, a week from Tuesday. I like the Brown Derby, when I have to eat out.

(*changing his mood*)

Otherwise I just as soon stay home and eat a hamburger, if we got a hamburger.

(*He takes off Tuxedo and puts jacket and pants back in the box, almost reverently.*)

JOHN (*aloud*): I gotta have it, and that's all there is to it.

(*He looks in the phone book, gets a number and dials it.*)

Hello, Pastorius? Me speak to Geoffrey. John J. Sullivan. Hello, Geoffrey?

Yeah, it just came. Fits absolutely perfect. Congratulations.

No, there's no hurry about the other stuff. I tell you what I wish you'd do, Geoffrey. I'm gonna be outa town for a couple months. I'm thinkin' of taking a trip to Florida, maybe Cuba. And from there I don't know where I'll go. A vacation, but not like the one I took at the taxpayers' expense, if you know what I mean.

No, I'm just gonna get some sunshine, lie on the beach and all that.

Ha ha. Well, yes I might even do that, Geoffrey.

So---will you have your fellow come here sometime and pick up the Tux. Then I'll send you my address where to mail it to me, and the other stuff I ordered.

All right, express. Either way.

And don't count on your money till this stuff begins to wear out.

Well, we done business together for a long time, Geoffrey.

Right. Right. Thank you. So long.

(*As he is concluding the conversation* MONA *enters quietly*

*and he turns toward her. Grinning, she is holding up the
cold cream jar, and he hangs up.*)

JOHN: You got it! Good work!

MONA: I was in and out of there so fast. If he'da been there he
couldn't have stopped me.

JOHN: Probably wouldn't want to stop a dame that only came to
swipe a jar of cold cream. He'd be glad to get rid of *that* screwball.
Are the goodies still there?

MONA: Just look.

(*She takes out a ring and a bracelet, smeared over with cold
cream. He picks up the pieces, one by one, with thumb and
forefinger.*)

JOHN: The fellow that bought you those sure had good taste.
And a bankroll.

(*reminiscing, picks up the ring and studies it*)

The dough for this, that was my end of the lease for a pier over
on the North River. Couple of Greek boys were having difficulty
leasing a pier, and they came to me.

(*holding up the bracelet*)

This was Arabian Tent money.

MONA: Arabian Tent money?

JOHN: Arabian Tent was a horse that paid thirty-to-one, and I had a
C-note on him to win. The fellow that gave me that tip never had
much luck himself, but he used to give me the long shots. He was a
clocker. Died of pneumonia.
We'll be back in the chips before long, don't worry.
My new Tuxedo came. I'm gonna have it sent out to the coast.
You wanta see how it looks on me?

MONA: If we have time.

JOHN: I'll just put on the coat. This fellow Geoffrey Pastorius, I'm

Far From Heaven

not an easy guy to fit, but I'll put him up against any tailor in the city. Or Lond, either. See how this collar fits me? Notice the sleeves.

(*He stands in momentary silent admiration of the coat.*)

I'll need this when we start going to those movie parties.

MONA: Well, I always did like you in a Tux.

JOHN: Yeah, you always said that.

MONA: What did you do with those studs I gave you?

JOHN: I loaned them to my brother Joe, but I'll get them back.

MONA: Well, do you think we ought to start going uptown?

JOHN (*to prolong his enjoyment*): You like my new Tux? You really like it?

(*She does not answer; she is distracted by the swift opening of the hall door. Her brother* WILLIE *is suddenly in the room, charged up from alcohol or drugs.*)

MONA (*alarmed*): Willie!

JOHN (*not alarmed*): Why hello Willie.

WILLIE (*taking a .38 from his pocket*): Get out of the way, you (*to* MONA).

(*He takes aim and fires at* JOHN, *who is sent backward by the impact of the bullet in his belly, and falls backward into a chair. He is almost immediately in dreadful pain and sleepy-eyed*).

JOHN: What's---that---for? Willie?

(*His head drops, but he raises it.*)

Who---paid---you---Willie?

(MONA *has run and knelt to protect* JOHN.)

WILLIE (*to* MONA): Get out of the way, or I'll give it to you too.

JOHN (*with an effort*): Fallon?

TWO BY O'HARA

(MONA *gets up, dashes toward* WILLIE, *who knocks her away, and fires again. This time* JOHN *slumps forward.* WILLIE *stares at him and* MONA *kneels before* JOHN *and takes his dead hand and holds it to her cheek. She looks up at her brother.*)

MONA: Go away, Willie.

WILLIE: He was no good, Mon'. He ruined you.

MONA (*quite gently*): Go on, go away, Willie.

WILLIE: He did, though. He rooonéd you.

(*He turns and she watches him, carefully putting his gun back in his pocket as he leaves. From then on she hardly ever takes her eyes off* JOHN. *She kisses his forehead, backs away still looking at him, opens his suitcase and begins to speak aloud.*)

MONA: . . . Out of the depth have I cried unto thee, O Lord. Lord hear my voice.
   Let thine ears be attentive to the voice of my supplication.
   If thou, O Lord, will mark iniquities, Lord, Lord, who shall stand it? For with thee there is mercy and plentiful redemption.

(*As she chants the prayer she finds and removes* JOHN's *.38 from the suitcase, and hugs it to her bosom. She starts her exit, and half way off she ceases to look at* JOHN. *She continues the prayer, numbly*):

MONA: My soul hath relied on His word, my soul hath hoped in the Lord. From the morning watch even to the night, let---

(*She is now through the door and out, and as the Curtain descends, with* JOHN *alone, the telephone begins to ring and continues to ring until the Curtain is complete.*)

THE END
1248   17 March 1962